San Francisco's 2010 World

GIANT SURPRISE

TRIUMPH
B O O K S

This book is available in quantity at special discounts for your group or organization. For further information contact:

Triumph Books
542 South Dearborn Street
Suite 750
Chicago, IL 60605
Phone: (312) 939-3330
Fax: (312) 663-3557
www.triumphbooks.com

Printed in the United States of America
ISBN: 978-1-60078-568-9

Content packaged by Mojo Media, Inc.
Joe Funk: Editor
Jason Hinman: Creative Director

All photographs courtesy of AP Images.

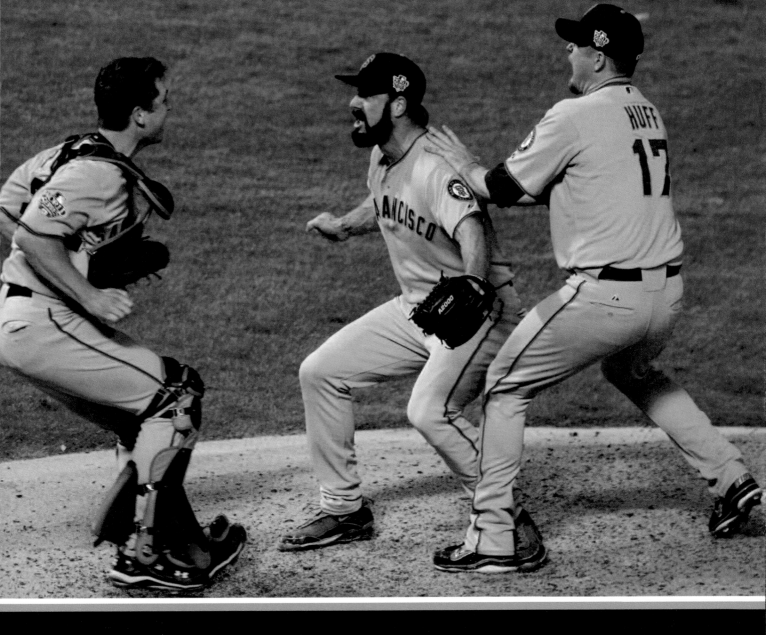

contents

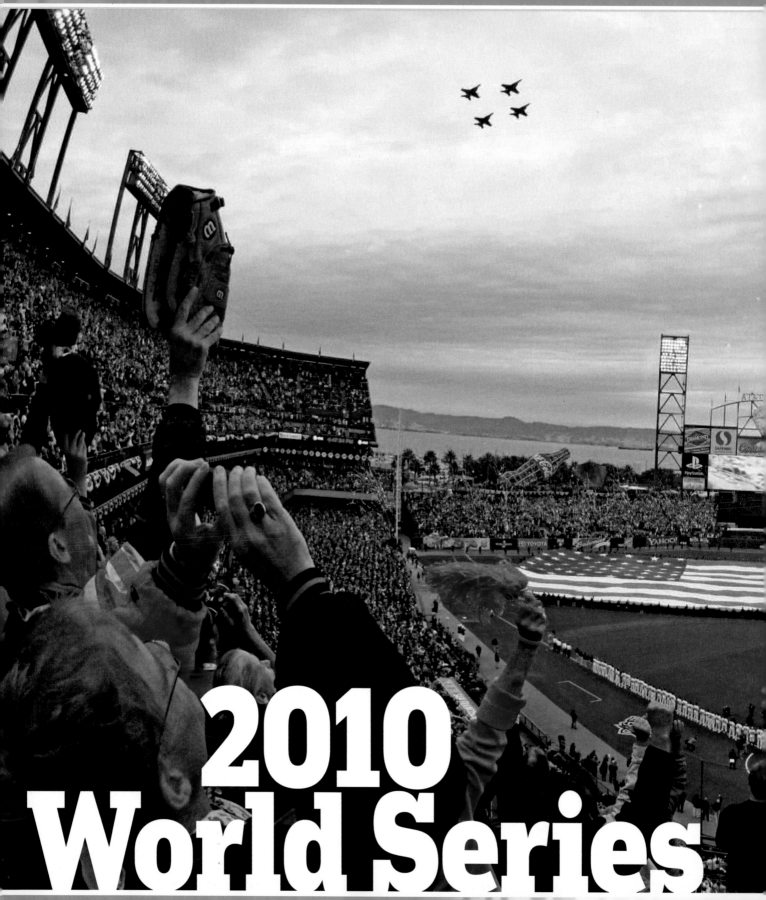

2010 World Series

World Series
Giants 11, Rangers 7

Game 1

Lincecum dominates, Giants rock Rangers' ace Lee to take Series opener

Game 1 of the 2010 World Series had all the trappings of a classic pitching duel between Cy Young Award winners Tim Lincecum and Cliff Lee.

During the 2010 playoffs, Lee had breezed through the batting orders of the Tampa Bay Rays and the New York Yankees, compiling a 3–0 record with a 0.75 ERA, and during his career he had a 7–0 record in eight postseason starts. In short, the Texas left-hander appeared to be unbeatable. Some of the pundits even went so far as to call him the best playoff pitcher ever. Yes, he looked that invincible. That is, until he toed the rubber at AT&T Park.

Texas got to Lincecum early, hanging a run on the Giants ace in each of the first two innings. The Rangers' quick start included a second-inning double by Lee. Despite allowing four hits, the situation could have been worse had Lincecum not effectively minimized the damage inflicted by the Rangers.

Freddy Sanchez's second double of the game drove home the Giants' first run in the third to end Lee's 16-inning postseason scoreless streak. Buster Posey doubled the damage with a two-bagger to drive home another run and tie the score at 2.

Lincecum and Lee then seemed to settle into their respective rhythms for a moment before the Giants teed off on Lee in the fifth.

Lincecum grounded out to start the inning before back-to-back doubles by Andres Torres and Sanchez—giving him three for the game—broke the tie. Lee recovered to strike out Buster Posey, but then he lost Pat Burrell to a walk and Cody Ross and Aubrey Huff followed with RBI singles.

By the time the Rangers recorded the third out of the fifth inning, the Giants had sent 11 batters to the plate, knocked Lee out of the game, and Juan Uribe had struck the inning's biggest blow with a three-run homer off Darren O'Day to push the Giants' lead to 8–2.

"I think more than anything it just goes to show you great pitchers sometimes they're a little bit off," said Bruce Bochy of Lee. "Hopefully when they are, you take advantage of mistakes, and we did it tonight. Again, it's quality at-bats—they mount up—

Game 1 of the World Series ended up not being the pitching match-up it was hyped to be. Both offenses kept putting runs on the board until the Giants came out on top 11–7.

and pitch count, things like that. But he's done a tremendous job for them. Again, he's the hottest pitcher in the postseason, but there's nothing that the hitters saw or anything. You know, he just probably wasn't quite hitting his spots like he normally does."

The Rangers scored two in the sixth to chase Lincecum, but the Giants added three in the eighth to push the lead to 11–4. The late runs gave the Giants some relief while withstanding a three-run ninth by the Rangers.

Not only did the victory give the Giants a 1–0 World Series lead it also placed a large amount of pressure on the shoulders of the Rangers since Lee had been considered a lock for a victory.

"Well, I saw the Giants work [Lee] pretty good," Rangers manager Ron Washington said. "You know, I think it was the third inning when he put the two runs up. He threw 32 pitches, just sort of ran out of gas there by the time we got to the fifth, and they put some good at-bats together, put some runs on the board, and we just couldn't recover."

Bochy's offense rarely splurged like it did in Game 1, leaving the Giants manager with the hope that the work his offense did against Lee would go a long way in the confidence department.

"Well, it is something that hopefully the hitters can build on," Bochy said. "You get confidence like that. We faced a great pitcher tonight and he wasn't quite on top of his game, and Timmy wasn't quite as sharp, either. It's not quite the game we thought it would be. But certainly a huge game for us, and we needed the runs.

"We had some great at-bats there, some two-out hits, and Juan's home run helped give us some cushion there. We're not a team that tries to slug it with other teams, but today they threw out some great at-bats." ■

An offensive onslaught by the Giants in the bottom of the fifth inning was capped off by a Juan Uribe three-run homer. The six runs scored in that bottom half of the inning gave the Giants a commanding lead.

World Series
Giants 9, Rangers 0

Game 2

Seven-run eighth inning sends Giants to Texas with two-game lead

A close ballgame turned into a rout for the Giants in Game 2 of the 2010 World Series when they defeated the Rangers 9–0.

Matt Cain started for the Giants and C.J. Wilson for the Rangers. Both had enjoyed success during the 2010 postseason and each appeared headed on their way to again keeping the hitters at bay when they locked up against each other.

Through the first sixth innings, the Giants scored the only run, which they managed in the fifth when Edgar Renteria hit a solo home run.

In the seventh, Wilson walked leadoff batter Cody Ross. The Rangers starter then left the game with a blister on a finger on his left hand. Darren Oliver replaced Wilson and retired Aubrey Huff on a groundout. Ross moved to second on the play, which allowed him to score the Giants' second run when Juan Uribe singled. While the Giants had a 2–0 lead, they were far from being in their comfort zone. That would change in the bottom of the eighth.

Darren O'Day struck out Andres Torres and Freddy Sanchez to start the inning before Buster Posey singled. Left-hander Derek Holland was then brought in to pitch to left-handed hitting Nate Schierholtz, and Holland walked him to put runners at first and second.

At this point, the Rangers' pitching staff turned into "The Gang that Couldn't Shoot Straight."

Holland issued four balls Ross to load the bases before walking Aubrey Huff to drive in the Giants' third run. Mark Lowe took over for Holland and continued the trend by walking Uribe to score another run before Renteria singled to left to drive home two more runs.

Michael Kirkman relieved Lowe and Aaron Rowand greeted him with a two-run triple. Mercifully, Torres' RBI double drove home the Giants' seventh and final run of the eighth inning.

Meanwhile, Cain brought his best stuff, holding the potent Rangers' lineup scoreless on four hits through 7-2/3 innings to pick up the win.

"Well, he commanded the fastball on both sides of the plate and really just—I mean, he executed his pitches," said Posey, the Giants rookie catcher

The Rangers looked to bounce back in Game 2, but behind a brilliant start by Matt Cain and an offense led by Edgar Renteria the Giants got on the plane to Texas with a 2-0 series lead.

about Cain. "He threw them where he wanted to. He was aggressive and was able to get some quick outs here early in the game and keep his pitch count down, and you saw him really bear down there in the second and third with one out, and really executed his pitches really well against [Nelson] Cruz and [Ian] Kinsler."

The Giants right-hander also used the spacious confines of AT&T to his advantage by getting 13 fly-outs. The closest the Rangers got to scoring against Cain came when Ian Kinsler opened the fifth by hitting an 0–2 pitch to deep center field for what appeared to be a home run. But the ball bounced the right way for the Giants as it hit the corner of the cushioning at the top of the wall and ricocheted back into Torres' glove. Instead of a home run, Kinsler came up with a double.

"I thought it was a home run," Cain said. "I saw it hit and I thought it hit something behind the wall and I thought it was a home run, so I cashed it in as one run. Then I saw that Torres had thrown it in and he was standing on second. From there I just said, hey, I've got to try to keep that guy there and we'll just get the next guy, see if we can get the next guy out and see how it works out."

Two games into the World Series and the Giants had outscored the Rangers by a margin of 20–7, which was totally out of character for the cardiac Giants, a team more accustomed to one-run

games. But Bruce Bochy was hardly complaining.

"Well, it's nice to do it a little bit easier," the Giants manager said. "As you know, we don't do things easy. Really, it was a tight game going into the eighth inning there. The big inning certainly helped. But every pitch, every play was so important there for the most part. Again, Matt, what a job he did. I thought Juan's hit really meant a lot, too. A one-run game, there's no margin of error. Two runs, it makes life a little bit easier, especially for the pitcher. He can afford to make a mistake."

With a 2–0 lead in the Series, the Giants had accomplished what they set off to do at home before heading to Rangers Ballpark in Arlington for Game 3.

"We're going to their place. They're going to be fired up," Huff said. "Their fans have been waiting a long time for this, too. They're going to be loud. So we have to go in there, take the first one and worry about the next one. All they have to do is win the next one and they're right back in it."

Cain added: "Yeah, we've put ourselves in a good situation. We're definitely going into their ballpark where they're going to feel more comfortable, just like we're confident playing here at home and we're used to the park. We've just got to take that confidence and some of the good approaches that we've had into these last two games and take them down to Texas with us." ■

Edgar Renteria and Juan Uribe celebrate after scoring during the eighth inning of Game 2.

World Series
Giants 2, Rangers 4

Game 3

Moreland's home run, Lewis' pitching too much for Giants as Rangers avoid sweep

Taking their 2–0 World Series lead to Texas, the Giants were not able to take a commanding leading in Game 3 on October 30, 2010, at Rangers Ballpark in Arlington with 52,419 watching.

At the end of the night, the Giants were 4–2 losers, but it wasn't the kind of loss that leaves a team seeking answers. The Giants played well and tried to mount a comeback, only to come up short.

Most of the Giants' problems in Game 3 could be attributed to Rangers starter Colby Lewis, who went through the Giants' order with relative ease, allowing just five hits in 7-2/3 innings. The only form of offense the Giants could generate against the right-hander came in the form of solo home runs by Cody Ross and Andres Torres in the seventh and eighth innings, respectively.

"I threw a lot of sliders," Lewis said. "I think it's a situation also with my breaking ball that worked well. Basically that was it. It was trying to command the fastball in and out. I felt like I was kind of peeling off, jerking the fastball and letting it not really commanding the inside fastball to lefties. It felt good to righties, but I couldn't get it in to lefties. But definitely the slider, I think, played a large part tonight."

Lewis limited the stress on Rangers manager Ron Washington by affording the Giants just two at-bats with runners in scoring position.

The first of those opportunities came in the first inning. Freddy Sanchez singled with one out before Buster Posey drew a two-out walk. Lewis then struck out Pat Burrell, which would be the first of Burrell's four strikeouts on the evening.

In the sixth, Aubrey Huff stroked a two-out double, but again, Lewis recovered nicely by striking out Posey on a called third strike.

"He didn't make too many mistakes," Posey said. "Even when he did, they were down in the zone. He changed speeds really well, moved the ball in and out. I don't think he missed on the plate very much."

Not until Lewis hit Huff with two outs in the eighth did Washington call upon his bullpen, which wasn't exactly a comforting thought given the Giants' seven-run eighth inning in Game 2. This

Edgar Renteria speaks with umpire Bill Miller after being called out on strikes in the third inning.

time the Rangers' bullpen came through.

First, Darren O'Day retired Buster Posey on a ground ball to end the eighth.

"He made a pretty good pitch," Bruce Bochy said. "We had a good hitter up there, it was a good battle. Went to a full count and he got him out. Last time Buster got a base hit up the middle. But that's a good match-up. It was a good game, exciting game. But their guys made pitches when they had to."

Neftali Feliz shut down the Giants in the ninth by striking out Burrell, retiring Ross on a fly out then striking out Juan Uribe to end the game. And the Rangers closer looked overpowering while getting the job done with his fastball getting clocked in the 98 mph range.

Despite the failures of the Rangers' bullpen in Game 2, Lewis said he had no concerns about handing over the game to the bullpen.

"I wasn't worried at all," Lewis said. "Those guys have been doing it all year. Nefti came in throwing 100, as he usually does, pounding the strike zone early, and put guys away with the big fastball.

Johnathan Sanchez started for the Giants and lasted just 4-2/3 innings. The big blow came in the second when the Giants southpaw allowed a three-run homer to the Rangers' No. 9 hitter, Mitch Moreland.

"That's the American League, and their guy got a big hit," said Bochy when asked about seeing a No. 9 hitter hit a bomb like Moreland's. "Sanchez was a pitch away from having a pretty good outing there, but he was getting out of that jam and just made a mistake. Settled in after that and was throwing the ball better, but that's what you deal with with a DH."

Josh Hamiliton added a solo home run off Sanchez in the bottom of the fifth. Sanchez then walked Vladimir Guerrero to earn an early hook.

While the Giants' loss was not catastrophic, it did leave some thoughts to ponder.

Of the previous teams that led a World Series by a 2–1 margin, they went on to go 41–40. However, of the 41 teams leading 2–1 who won Game 4 to improve to a 3–1 Series lead, 35 went on to win the Series. Meanwhile, of the 40 teams that led 2–1 and failed to win Game 4, only 18 won the Series.

"Well, I feel great," Washington said. "We wanted to get back home. We felt comfortable here. We knew we could finally put a good game together, and we did. You know, it took the whole team to get it done, and they certainly did. But it feels great. You know, we have to come back tomorrow and do the same thing." ■

Jonathan Sanchez's nine-pitch sequence to Mitch Moreland in the bottom of the second ended in a three-run home run and a Texas lead.

World Series
Giants 4, Rangers 0

Game 4

Bumgarner youngest pitcher to collect World Series win in 29 years.

Throughout the regular season as well as the postseason, all talk about the Giants' starting staff focused on Tim Lincecum and Matt Cain. Enter Madison Bumgarner.

Given the responsibility of silencing the Rangers in Game 4 of the World Series, the 21-year-old left-hander answered the challenge with a vintage performance on Halloween night at Rangers Ballpark in Arlington with 51,920 watching. Among those attending were former presidents George W. Bush and George H.W. Bush, who took care of the ceremonial first pitch to Hall of Famer Nolan Ryan, now the president of the Rangers.

Bumgarner, who was too young to have voted for either of the previous Presidents, led the way for the Giants as he blanked the Rangers for eight innings, allowing just three hits while striking out six to collect the victory in a 4–0 Giants win.

Bumgarner, who began the season at Triple A Fresno, became the youngest pitcher to claim a win in the World Series since Fernando Valenzuela turned the trick against the Yankees in Game 3 of

the 1981 World Series.

Bumgarner, who played high school baseball in North Carolina, had noted prior to his start that the World Series could not bring any more pressure than trying to win the North Carolina state championship. He looked cool enough throughout the game that such sentiments were actually believable.

"Sounds ridiculous, but at the time as a high school player that's the biggest game I had played in," Bumgarner said. "Now obviously this is way bigger. It's the World Series, the biggest game you're going to play in. I try to just go out there and tell myself it's just another game, though, and look back on it after it's over with, and hopefully it was a good result."

The Rangers did little against the southpaw, failing to get a runner into scoring position until the seventh inning when Josh Hamilton reached on an error with one out and moved to second when Nelson Cruz singled with two outs to bring always dangerous Ian Kinsler to the plate. At the time, the Giants held a 3–0 lead, so a bomb by Kinsler would

The Giants were back to their winning ways in Game 4 behind solid starting pitching and home runs from Aubrey Huff and Buster Posey. With the win they took a commanding 3-1 lead in the Series with one more game to be played in Texas.

have tied the game. Cooly, Bumgarner got Kinsler to fly out to left to end the threat.

"Just keep telling myself to relax," Bumgarner said when asked about how he managed to remain calm during the game. "And I've told myself so much that it's starting to become second nature, and it makes it a lot easier on me and the players, I think, to see somebody that's relaxed out there throwing. That's it, I guess."

As good as Bumgarner was, Bochy elected to lift him after eight innings and 106 pitches to bring in closer Brian Wilson. "I talked to Buster [Posey] when he came back after the eighth, and he wasn't quite as sharp in that inning," Bochy said. "He did his job. Wilson hadn't thrown in a while. And that kid, I can't say enough about what he did tonight. I mean, 21-year-old kid on that stage pitching like that. He had it all working."

Wilson pitched a perfect ninth to complete the Giants' second shutout of the Series and fourth of the postseason.

Aubrey Huff had the big blow for the Giants on offense. Comfortable in the designated hitter role after years of playing in the American League, Huff relinquished his first base duties to serve as the DH in Game 4. He connected for a two-run homer in the third off Rangers starter Tommy Hunter to give the Giants a 2–0 lead.

Huff grew up a Rangers fan while living in the Dallas–Fort Worth area, which made the moment all the more memorable.

"It's certainly special," Huff said. "Haven't played these guys, normally we would play these guys before the Series started. It's in the back of your mind you'd like to hit a big homer to put you ahead. It's pretty surreal right now. Again, we've got a lot of work to do tomorrow. But definitely that was a big turning point of the game with Colby Lewis the way he threw yesterday just getting ahead, and Hunter is the same type of pitcher. To be able to get the lead, we can be a little bit more aggressive. Certainly special for me no doubt."

Andres Torres had three hits, including an RBI double in the seventh and Posey added a home run in the eighth to build the four-run cushion.

The Giants' victory put the team in unfamiliar territory with a 3–1 edge in the Series and perched on the brink of winning the franchise's first World Series since moving from New York to San Francisco in 1958. Forty-four previous Series participants held 3–1 leads and they finished what they started 38 times.

"It's a good spot to be in, no doubt," Huff said. "But we had a 3–1 lead against the Phillies and they came back and beat us a tough game at our place and we had to go back and really grind out a Game 6, and didn't really want to go to Game 7. [Leading] 3–1 is great, but this is the playoffs, and teams are certainly capable of winning three straight. We've got to go out there tomorrow and get back to work, act like we're down 1–3." ■

Rookie starting pitcher Madison Bumgarner quieted the Rangers' bats at home to collect the win in Game 4, scattering three hits and two walks over eight innings pitched.

World Series
Giants 3, Rangers 1

Game 5

Behind Lincecum, Giants bring home
San Francisco's first-ever Series title

Candlestick Park came and went without a World Series champion. "The Say Hey Kid," "The Dominican Dandy," "Cha-Cha," and "Stretch" all wore Giants uniforms and never won a World Series while in San Francisco.

You could say the City by the Bay was due.

All it took was a cast of misfits and a five-star pitching staff to bring an end to the drought of not winning a World Series that dated back to 1954, when the Giants still played at the Polo Grounds and wore New York across the chests of their uniforms.

Giants manager Bruce Bochy was six months old when the Giants claimed their last World Series, *I Love Lucy* was the top ranked TV show, a gallon of gas cost 21 cents, and Dwight D. Eisenhower was President.

So let it be known that on November 1, 2010, the Giants defeated the Texas Rangers 3–1 in Game 5 of the 2010 World Series to become world champions.

"They did all right," Bochy said. "I couldn't be prouder of the group. Just shows you what a team can do when it plays together...these players accepted their roles and they had one mission and that was to win. And they got it done."

The deciding game began as the pitching duel between Tim Lincecum and Cliff Lee that had been anticipated for Game 1. Both pitchers put up zeroes through the first six innings, with Lincecum holding the Rangers hitless through three innings before Michael Young finally ended the suspense with a single through the middle.

The seventh inning brought another story.

Cody Ross singled off Lee to open the top of the seventh. Juan Uribe followed suit with another single through the middle to put runners at first and second for Aubrey Huff, which brought an interesting decision for Bruce Bochy: Should he get Huff to move the runners into scoring position with a sacrifice bunt—for slumping Pat Burrell, or should he swing away?

Huff bunted and accomplished what he set out to do when Lee fielded the bunt and threw to first, bringing Burrell to the plate with two runners in scoring position.

With a dominating start from Tim Lincecum, the Giants won their first World Series title since uprooting from New York and moving to San Francisco.

Burrell walked to the plate having struck out nine times in 11 at-bats during the Series. The count moved to 3–2 then Lee pulled the string with a wicked cutter that Burrell swung at and missed.

Edgar Renteria brought the final hurdle that Lee needed to clear to escape the inning. The Rangers left-hander fell behind 2–0 in the count then threw a cutter that caught too much of the plate. Renteria swung and sent a ball to left field that ducked into the stands for a three-run homer to put the Giants up 3–0.

Ross jumped up and down when he landed on home plate. Once Renteria reached the dugout, Burrell embraced Renteria for getting the job done that he could not.

But there was still work to do if the Giants wanted to finish off the mission they began during their National League Division Series with the Atlanta Braves and carried through their National League Championship Series with the Philadelphia Phillies to reach the World Series.

Lincecum seemed to sense the moment by striking out Vladimir Guerrero. Nelson Cruz then got the Rangers on the scoreboard with a home run to left field. Lincecum followed by walking Kinsler, which teased the Rangers that something might be brewing. Instead, Lincecum slammed the door, striking out David Murphy and Bengie Molina to end the threat.

"You could see it in the first inning," Giants catcher Buster Posey said. "He had late action on his fastball. He had that look about him. He had that confidence."

Hoping to keep the Giants from adding on to their lead, Rangers manager Ron Washington called on closer Neftali Feliz to replace Lee, and he successfully retired the Giants in the eighth and ninth innings.

Meanwhile, Lincecum retired the Rangers in order in the eighth on a strikeout and two ground-outs before giving way to Brian Wilson in the ninth.

Dangerous Josh Hamilton led off the inning against Wilson, and the Giants bearded wonder caught Hamilton looking at strike three for the first out. Guerrero then grounded out to Renteria at shortstop to bring up Cruz.

With the tension building and more than 50 years of frustration behind the Giants' organization, Wilson struck out Cruz swinging to end the game and set off a celebration on the Texas infield.

"Oh my goodness, feels amazing," Wilson said. "To lead up to this moment, what a battle, for fans to come out in October and just go nuts, that was October for us."

Lincecum grabbed the win, living the dream by getting the job done in the deciding game of the World Series. When asked about fulfilling the dream of youngsters from coast to coast, Linceum quipped: "Usually I dreamed about being the hitter, but in this case I'll take it." ■

Edgar Renteria's three-run homer in the top of the seventh inning was all Tim Lincecum and Brian Wilson needed to secure the Giants' first World Series title since 1954.

Renteria World Series MVP

Shortstop enters elite class with second Series-winning hit...13 years after first

Game 5 of the 2010 World Series could have gone either way, but Edgar Renteria made sure it went the Giants' way.

Renteria delivered a three-run homer in the deciding game to lead the Giants to their first championship since 1954, and the veteran shortstop took home Most Valuable Player honors as a result.

Renteria's home run came against Rangers starter Cliff Lee in the seventh inning, giving the Giants all the runs they needed in their 3–1 win to earn their fourth victory in the best of seven series.

Renteria hit .411 (7–17) with two home runs and six RBIs during the Series, again finding the spotlight in the Fall Classic. Thirteen years earlier he had the game-winning hit for the Florida Marlins in Game 7 of the 1997 World Series. By getting his second winning hit in two different World Series, Renteria became the fourth player in major league history to do so, joining Joe DiMaggio, Lou Gehrig, and Yogi Berra.

In addition to his Game 5 heroics, Renteria also stepped forward in Game 2 with a solo home run in the fifth inning that started the Giants scoring, and he added a two-run single in the game that turned into a 9–0 Giants rout.

Renteria struggled with injuries all season, serving three different stints on the disabled list. Nevertheless, the Giants made sure he was active for the postseason.

"It was a tough year for me," Renteria said following the game, "but I told myself to keep working hard...because something is going to be good this year for you.... I feel proud for myself, I feel proud for my teammates."

After accepting the trophy recognizing him as the fifth shortstop to be named World Series MVP, Renteria said winning the World Series was, "very satisfying for me."

"They have faith in me and give me a chance to play in the playoffs and everything go well," Renteria said.

Prior to his memorable at-bat against Lee, Renteria joked with Andres Torres that he would hit one out.

"I got confidence in me, but I was joking like

I'm going to get it out," Renteria said. "But it went out. But I got confident, looking for one pitch, and if he throws I'm going to hit it back to the middle. So he tried to throw the cutter, and the cutter stay in the middle and that's why it go out."

Renteria said the homer brought him a great feeling.

"But I no forget we play against a great offensive team like Texas," Renteria said. "That's why I told my teammates, keep playing, keep playing, keep [concentrating] because we know they can tie the game right away. So teammates did a great job, and that's why we win."

When asked if the 2010 winner was bigger than 1997's, Renteria answered: "No, both is the same feeling, same emotions, same feeling. It's unbelievable. It's unbelievable being in that situation, and I enjoyed both World Series." ■

Edgar Renteria joins Lou Gehrig, Joe DiMaggio, and Yogi Berra as the only players to deliver the game-winning hits in two different World Series clinching games. Keeping that kind of company is deserving of a World Series MVP.

Building the 2010 Team

Sabean's mix of rookies and journeymen just what the Giants needed

The 2010 San Francisco Giants have been like Forrest Gump's box of chocolates. When you mix a bunch of castoffs, you never know what you're going to get.

Giants general manager Brian Sabean somehow found enough chemistry and talent among players—who for the most part other teams did not want—to ride the group to a World Series championship.

It started when he signed Aubrey Huff during the offseason. Next up was an early-season pickup of Pat Burrell. Sabean then decided to call up two top prospects from Triple-A Fresno—catcher Buster Posey and left-hander Madison Bumgarner. He finished his masterpiece—which many would have considered a velvet Elvis at the time—by blocking Cody Ross from going to San Diego and bringing the veteran aboard.

Huff and Burrell combined to hit 44 home runs and drive in 137 runs during the regular season; neither player was exactly a hot commodity when the Giants acquired him.

Huff had split time between Baltimore and Detroit in 2009 and managed to produce just 15 home runs. Meanwhile, Burrell's time with the Tampa Bay Rays had been a disaster. In 146 games over two seasons with the Rays, Burrell hit just 21 home runs before the Rays released him in May. Burrell responded to the wake-up call with 18 home runs for the Giants in 96 games.

In addition to performing on the field, both players were positive additions to the clubhouse, Huff bringing his acerbic wit and Burrell his veteran leadership.

Huff attributes his sense of humor in the clubhouse to his beginning in the major leagues when veteran players rode him hard, which he says did nothing to help him perform. He made a note to himself back then that he would not assume the same character once he became a clubhouse veteran, and he hasn't.

Posey and Bumgarner have been splendid, both seemingly headed for future greatness. But hand it to Sabean for having enough foresight to trade veteran catcher Bengie Molina to the Rangers to make

way for Posey, which many felt was a risky move and a lot of pressure to place on the young catcher.

Finally, there's Ross. Had there been a Most Valuable Player award for the National League Division Series, the veteran would have been the likely choice. He drove home the only run in Game 1, and he homered and drove home the winning run in Game 4, which clinched the Series for the Giants.

"You know, we all just came together," Ross said. "And we had one thing in mind, and that was to win. We all had to check our ego[s] at the door and put the personal statistics aside and go out there and just play as a team, and I think that's one of the main reasons we're at where we are now. Obviously our pitching is outstanding. But for us to come together and play well as a team, it says a lot."

Burrell added: "It's easy for guys to come together when everyone has the same goal. And that's obviously to win. So we made—there's a lot of guys here that didn't start the year here that are big parts of this team. And like I said, when everybody's going out there to win, it makes a big difference." ■

Cody Ross hits a double during the second inning of Game 2.

Tim Lincecum

The Freak leads baseball's best pitching staff

"The Freak" is unique and San Francisco's very own to embrace. Without the diminutive right-hander, the Giants would not be World Series champions.

Among the endearing traits of Tim Lincecum, a.k.a. The Freak, is the dark long hair that makes him look like he's either into Goth or grunge. In addition, he's superstitious, which has led to him wearing the same Giants hat since his rookie season, thereby explaining why the thing resembles a cap worn in a rain storm and dried in a dessert. Giants fans relate to Lincecum, which can be seen in the T-shirts that say "The Freak" on them or the wigs fans wear to the games.

"It's a really good atmosphere, a lot of people as far as the shirts go, kind of like I said, talking about before, kind of embracing me, kind of it is what it is kind of thing," said Lincecum of the attention. "I'm having fun with it. You see all the Pablo hats or the Panda hats and the Brian Wilson 'fear the beard' shirts and things. Just something for them to play on and have fun with, and it's good. I think it gets them

involved, and I feel like they're part of the team".

While Lincecum is truly a quirky character somewhat off the beaten path, his most endearing trait is the fact he's one of the best pitchers in the major leagues.

Though Lincecum stands just 5'11" and weighs 172 pounds, he makes due with his technique and repertoire of pitches, which includes a mid-90s fastball, a changeup, a curve, and a slider.

The Cubs drafted Lincecum in the 48th round of the 2003 draft out of high school in Renton, Washington, but he opted to attend the University of Washington. In his first year pitching for the Huskies he won Pac-10 Freshman of the Year and Pitcher of the Year honors. In 2006, he won the Golden Spikes Award, which is awarded to the top amateur baseball player for that season. And Lincecum had quite a season in 2006 when he went 12–4 with a 1.94 ERA and 199 strikeouts in 125-1/3 innings.

In 2005, he again was drafted, this time by the Cleveland Indians. Again, he did not sign. Not until the Giants selected him with the 10th pick of the

Two-time Cy Young Award winner Tim Lincecum was again the ace of the Giants pitching staff in 2010. His staff-best record of 16 wins and 10 losses was key to the team's success.

"It's a really good atmosphere...I feel like they're part of the team."

—Tim Lincecum on the fans and how they pick up the players' quirky characteristics

2006 draft did he sign a professional contract, which he did on June 30, 2006, agreeing to a deal that paid him a $2.025 million signing bonus.

After Russ Ortiz suffered an injury early in the 2007 season, Lincecum was called to the major leagues and made his first start on May 6, when he received a no-decision against the Philadelphia Phillies.

He made his second career start on May 11, 2007, in Denver against the Colorado Rockies and came away with his first win after allowing two earned runs in seven innings. He would finish his rookie season with a 7–5 record with a 4.00 ERA in 24 starts.

In his second season in the major leagues, Lincecum continued to turn up the heat. In eight of his starts he had double-digit strikeouts, finishing the season with 265 strikeouts in 227 innings to lead the National League while going 18–5 with a 2.62 ERA. Included in his totals were two complete games. At the end of the season, Lincecum was named the recipient of the 2008 National League Cy Young Award. By winning the award, he became first second-year player to win the award since Bret Saberhagen and Dwight Gooden, of the Kansas City Royals and New York Mets, respectively, won the American League and National League awards in 1985.

In 2009, Lincecum again dominated National League hitters, posting a 15–7 record with 261 strikeouts in 225-1/3 innings. Once again the Baseball Writers Association of America voted Lincecum as the winner of the National League Cy Young Award, earning him the distinction of being the first to win the Cy Young in his first two full seasons in the major leagues.

Lincecum did not have his best season with the Giants in 2010, but he still managed to post a 16–10 record with a 3.43 ERA and he pitched 212-1/3 innings, surpassing the 200 innings mark for the third consecutive season, which is a blue-collar badge of honor for a major league starting pitcher. In addition, he went 5–1 with a 1.94 ERA in six September starts to help lead his team down the stretch toward a National League West title, thereby putting the team in line for its incredible playoff run. ■

Striking out almost 10 batters every nine innings, Lincecum's staff-leading 231 K's helped the Giants lead all National League teams in strike outs during the 2010 season.

Buster Posey

Catcher starts 2010 in Triple A, finishes batting cleanup in World Series

Sometimes a team gets an unexpected lift that can help them reach a place where they did not believe they could go.

Buster Posey did that for the Giants in 2010.

Posey proved to be everything and more than he was cracked up to be when the Giants made him the fifth overall selection of the 2008 draft.

Posey had been in the spotlight for a long time by the time the Giants brought him into the fold, dating as far back as his high school days.

Posey attended Lee County High School in Leesburg, Georgia, where he was recognized as the Georgia Gatorade Player of the Year, Louisville Slugger State Player of the Year, and an EA Sports All-American. He accepted a baseball scholarship to Florida State University and initially played shortstop for the Seminoles as a freshman, starting every game en route to earning Louisville Slugger Freshman All-American honors.

The FSU coaching staff opted to move Posey to catcher for his sophomore season and he continued to thrive, hitting .382 while playing flawlessly behind the plate. By the time he had completed his junior season, Posey had hit .463 with 26 home runs and 93 RBIs en route to winning the Golden Spikes Award, the award given to the player recognized as the best in amateur baseball.

Posey signed with the Giants after receiving a $6.2 million bonus and the Giants invited him to spring training in 2009. By the end of that season he made his major league debut with the team, playing in 17 games in September.

Determined not to rush their top prospect, the Giants had him start the 2010 season at Fresno, where he hit .349 in 47 games before getting called up to the Giants on May 29. The following day, Posey went 3–4 with three RBIs and his career was off and running. Playing against the Cincinnati Reds on June 9, he hit his first major league home run against Aaron Harang.

Posey played mostly at first base through June before the Giants traded Bengie Molina to the Texas Rangers on June 30, putting Posey behind the plate. The move did nothing to thwart Posey's

The highly anticipated arrival of Posey on May 29th was a good one. In his debut, he went 3–4 at the plate with three RBIs, helping the Giants beat the Diamondbacks 12–1.

Posey finished his rookie season with a .305 batting average, 18 home runs, and 67 RBIs—and a 2010 World Series ring.

offense. He connected for his first career grand slam on July 7 against the Milwaukee Brewers in a game that saw him hit another home run and collect four hits along with six RBIs.

Posey showed just how hot he could be by going through a 10-game stretch in which he hit .514 with 19 hits, six home runs, and 13 RBIs. Included in Posey's torrid July was a 21-game hitting streak, which left him a game shy of tying Willie McCovey's rookie record.

Posey took over the Giants' cleanup spot in the order and held his own.

His eighth-inning home run against the Chicago Cubs at Wrigley Field gave the Giants a 1–0 win. On the final day of the season, Posey hit his 18th home run of the season, which also came in the eighth inning, to help lead the Giants to a win over the San Diego Padres, which earned the Giants the National League West pennant.

Posey finished his rookie season with a .305 batting average, 18 home runs, and 67 RBIs. No doubt a great career awaits. ■

Posey's final stat line of 18 home runs, 67 RBIs, and a .305 batting average shows that his No. 1 organizational prospect rating heading into the 2010 season was well deserved.

Matt Cain

Tough-luck No. 2 starter helps reverse San Francisco's fortunes

Ever since joining the Giants in 2005, Matt Cain has earned his reputation as a bulldog. Standing 6'3" and weighing 235 pounds, the right-hander who hails from Germantown, Tennessee, became the first pick of the Giants in 2002 (25th overall) and after a quick trip through the Giants' farm system, he made his major league debut at the age of 20 on August 25, 2002, against the Colorado Rockies. He pitched well—allowing just three hits and two runs in five innings—but he took the loss.

Nevertheless, he joined the Giants' starting rotation and he picked up his first win in the big leagues on September 4, 2002, against the Arizona Diamondbacks. Five days later he pitched a complete-game two hitter against the Chicago Cubs.

Since then all Cain has done is log innings and put away hitters.

After accruing 46-1/3 innings in his rookie season, Cain has compiled season innings totals of 190-2/3, 200, 217-2/3, 217-2/3, and 223-1/3, proving that a pitcher can have quality stuff and be a workhorse.

Included in Cain's pitching repertoire are three quality pitches, including a 93 mph fastball, a changeup, and a curveball. Bruce Bochy attributed Cain's improvement over the years to the right-hander finding better command of his pitches.

"That's what's made him a different pitcher, I think," Bochy said. "He has evolved to a complete pitcher from what he was at a younger age when he was pretty much a power guy. He's got a good slider, curveball, and change-up. He has good command of them, and when he does, that's when he pitches well."

Unfortunately for Cain, he hasn't always had the backing of a quality bullpen nor a quality offense during his career, which enlightens those who wonder how such a talented pitcher could have a 57–62 career record. Then again, he does have a 3.45 career earned run average.

How has Cain keep his sanity in the past given the lack of backing he received?

"We've always felt like we had a good group of guys here ever since I've been here," Cain said.

An ace on just about any other staff, Matt Cain was the solid "2" of the Giants 1–2 punch at the top of their rotation's throughout the 2010 season. Cain owned the rotations best ERA at 3.14 and lead the team in innings pitched with 223-1/3.

"We've had our tough times, and we've always gone through our good spurts and our bad spurts. But obviously this year has changed where we've gone through our bad spurts but haven't worried about it, just popped right back out of it whereas in years past we might have sat in those ruts for a little bit longer. I think that's what has made this year special. But it's also helped, I think, a ton of us to get out of those ruts this year because of stuff we've gone through in the past."

In addition, receiving little run support and always pitching in close games has helped his development.

"I think you just learn to maybe slow some of the key situations in the game down," Cain said. "You try to take advantage of taking control of the game when you know you may have guys on base. And counts aren't in your favor or whatever. You just try to figure out ways to slow the game down to get back to the pace that you want it to be at to try to get the momentum back on your side instead of the hitter's advantage."

Cain proved to be at his best in Game 2 of the 2010 World Series when he got the win in a 9–0 Giants rout after pitching 7-2/3 innings and holding the Rangers to no runs on four hits.

Cain experienced a breakthrough season in 2009 when he went 14–8 with a 2.89 ERA along with 171 strikeouts. Based on the Giants' success in 2010, and the fact Cain posted a 13–11 record with a 3.14 ERA, baseball fans might be seeing just the beginning for an emerging star. ■

Matt Cain was almost perfect in the 2010 postseason. In his 21-1/3 innings pitched over three starts he won two games, allowed no earned runs, and struck out 13.

Cody Ross

Late-season pickup's dramatic postseason homers carry Giants to Series

Long before Cody Ross ever dreamed of becoming a major league baseball player he longed to be, of all things, a rodeo clown.

Ross' father was in the rodeo and up until the age of 10, Ross thought he would be a rodeo clown, which he attributed to the fact he was drawn to the fearlessness of the rodeo clowns.

Alas, Ross, who grew up in New Mexico, was chosen by the Detroit Tigers in the fourth round of the 1999 draft.

By 2003, Ross was in the major leagues with the Tigers, who traded him to the Los Angeles Dodgers prior to the 2004 season, and thus he began the life of a major league journeyman.

In Ross' seven major league seasons, he played for the Tigers, Dodgers, Reds, and Marlins before the Giants picked him up off waivers on August 22, 2010.

Upon moving to the Giants, Ross met with general manager Brian Sabean, who told him the Giants had acquired him because they were trying to win. Their reasons for getting him were not to keep the first-place San Diego Padres from claiming him.

Ross told Sabean he would do whatever it took to help the team win. Then he went out and backed up his words for the remainder of the season. In addition to blending in well in the clubhouse, Ross played all three outfield positions and had an .819 OPS for the Giants. He hit .288 with three homers and seven RBIs in 33 games.

However, he saved his best work for the postseason and, in particular, the National League Division Series.

In the Giants' clinching Game 4 win, Ross hit a solo home run off Braves starter Derek Lowe that broke up a no-hitter and tied the game. Then he delivered the game-winning hit when he singled in the seventh.

Ross' work gave him three RBIs for the NLDS. His Game 1 RBI proved special since no other player in baseball history had so few RBIs for a team in the regular season and registered a postseason RBI, according to the Elias Sports Bureau.

"What a great addition for us, for this ballclub," Giants manager Bruce Bochy said. "He plays both

Cody Ross was acquired by the San Francisco Giants via a waiver claim at the end of August. Even though his time with the Giants in 2010 has been short lived, he became a big contributor in the postseason.

sides of the ball so well, and the big hits he's gotten—I mean, Lowe is throwing the ball so well, he made it look easy out there, and Cody hit the home run. It just seemed like he charged up the ballclub, and of course he got another hit [to win the game]."

Ross followed his success against the Braves by coming up big against the Phillies in the National League Championship Series. In 20 at-bats, he hit .350 with three home runs, three doubles, and five RBIs to win MVP honors. ∎

Ross's five home runs and .294 average throughout the 2010 postseason were key to the Giants' offensive success in all three postseason Series.

Aubrey Huff

Veteran first baseman leads Giants with humor, home runs

Aubrey Huff found a home in San Francisco when the former outcast for several organizations became a treasure for the Giants in 2010.

After playing for the Tampa Bay Devil Rays, Houston Astros, Baltimore Orioles, and Detroit Tigers, Huff found a home with the Giants and led the team with a .290 batting average, 26 home runs, and 86 RBIs.

Huff came to the Giants via a one-year deal he agreed to with the team on January 10, 2010, that paid him $3 million.

In addition to Huff's baseball skills, he brought a good presence to the clubhouse, where he is a noted prankster with an acerbic wit.

"I've always been the kind of guy that likes to turn it up a little bit in the clubhouse, keep it loose," Huff said. "I don't care if you're a veteran or a younger guy, if you're having fun in the clubhouse and everybody is having a good time and everybody really starts caring for each other, and I think that has a lot to do with winning on the field. I don't think you can actually play baseball without a good group of guys that mix well together."

Among the highlights from Huff's season was his first career inside-the-park home run against the Pittsburgh Pirates on April 14, 2010. Huff also came to be known for coming up with a red "Rally Thong" (see the Rally Thong feature in this book).

Throughout the Giants' run to their World Series championship, Huff embodied the spirit of the team and came through with many big hits. And he was rewarded for his play and his spirit by playing for a winner for the first time in his 11-year career.

Ironically, the team the Giants defeated in the World Series, the Texas Rangers, was Huff's favorite team as a youngster growing up in Mineral Wells, Texas.

Huff attended Vernon College in North Texas before transferring to the University of Miami prior to his junior season. While playing for the Hurricanes, *Baseball Weekly* named Huff a second team All-American after he set a Miami season record with 95 RBIs.

The Devil Rays drafted Huff in the fifth round of the 1998 draft, and he made his major league debut in 2000. ■

Pat Burrell celebrates with Juan Uribe after scoring on an RBI single by Aubrey Huff during the sixth inning of Game 1.

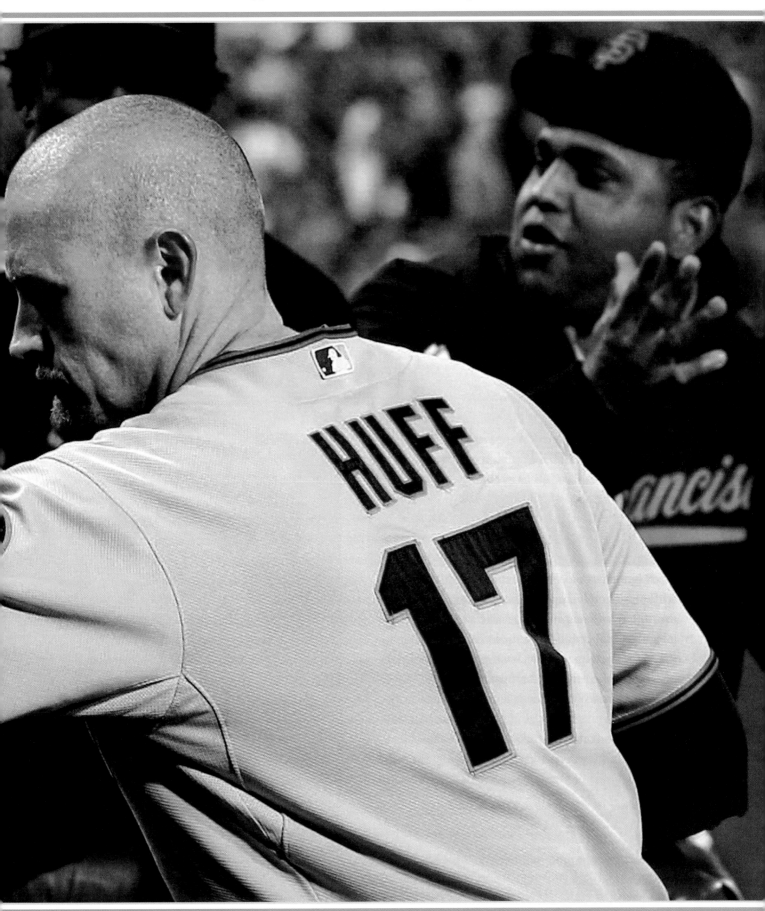

Huff's Rally Thong

Lacy undergarment proves to be Giants' good luck charm

Talk about taking the superstition thing a little too far.... No sport has players who fall prey to superstition as easily as baseball. Hall of Famer Wade Boggs ate chicken every day because he bought into the idea that eating chicken gave him good karma. Others have lucky charms and lucky routines.

But Aubrey Huff brought out a new one toward the end of the 2010 season, and if one is indeed superstitious, Huff's practice of wearing a particular undergarment had a lot to do with the Giants becoming the champions of baseball.

Huff began wearing a lacy, red and black piece of PAPI brand underwear, which he has proudly modeled while strolling around the Giants' clubhouse before and after games. Since he began with his fashion statement, that particular piece of underwear has come to be known as the "Rally Thong."

Huff's wife, Baubi, bought the thong for her husband as a joke several years ago. After seeing it in one of his drawers this season, he figured he'd take it to work and wear it for a few laughs while lightening the mood in the clubhouse.

To the credit of the Giants first baseman, he took one for the team by employing the somewhat different choice of underwear beginning with 30 games left on the 2010 schedule. To Huff's way of thinking this was strictly a team gesture—he did not begin the practice to end a batting slump, he did so to give the team good luck. And he figured that the "Rally Thong" would be worth at least 20 wins in the Giants' final thirty games, which would therefore lead the team to a National League West pennant.

The club got off to a 3–1 start with Huff in the "Rally Thong" and he began to gain believers in the power of the thong.

Huff has always been known for his clubhouse antics and has never minded making himself the

object of the joke. One can only imagine how ridiculous Huff looked talking to reporters wearing only his thong—actually one would probably not want to imagine such a sight.

Given the results, Giants fans would probably declare Huff the fashion plate of recent Giants teams. On August 30 the Giants trailed the first-place San Diego Padres by five games. The next night Huff went with his new look, and over the final 30 games of the season, the Giants won 20 to

win the division just as Huff forecast.

Huff has since received three large boxes of thongs from PAPI that he shared with his teammates.

Giants manager Bruce Bochy declared that he did not really like seeing Huff parading around in the thong, but he couldn't argue with the results.

That is one powerful thong. ■

The superstitious antics of Aubrey Huff (right) in the Giants clubhouse may not be G-(string) rated, but you cannot argue with the Rally Thong's record.

Edgar Renteria

Oft-injured shortstop once again finds himself in the postseason

Coming up big has been Edgar Renteria's trademark since he first arrived to the major leagues with the Florida Marlins in 1996.

The shortstop from Barranquilla, Colombia, had a penchant for playing well in the clutch. Personifying that trait was Renteria's work in the 1997 World Series when the Florida Marlins played the Cleveland Indians.

With the home crowd roaring in the bottom of the 11th inning of Game 7, Renteria stepped to the plate to face Indians right-hander Charles Nagy with two outs and the bases loaded. He then delivered what they wanted to see: a base hit through the middle of the infield.

And just like that, the Marlins had their first world championship and Renteria was forever minted as one of the game's top clutch players.

The Marlins traded Renteria to the Cardinals prior to the 1999 season and he continued to be a winner. Entering the 2010 postseason, Renteria had played on six playoff teams in 15 major league seasons, serving stints for the Marlins, Cardinals, Red Sox, Braves, and Tigers before signing to play for the Giants on December 4, 2008.

Along the way, Renteria made five All-Star teams and won two Gold Gloves.

However, in two seasons with the Giants, he has played in just 196 games, being somewhat limited by injuries, particularly during the 2010 season when he missed 14 games with a groin injury, 20 games with a hamstring injury, 19 with a biceps injury, and 10 with an elbow injury.

Obviously, Renteria no longer is the dazzling kid that arrived in the major leagues at the age of 22. However, he still has his moments, and one of those came in Game 2 of the 2010 World Series almost 13 years to the day that he hit his walk-off single to win the 1997 World Series.

Facing tough Texas left-hander C.J. Wilson, Renteria connected with a 91 mph fastball and deposited the baseball over the left-field wall of AT&T Park to give the Giants a 1–0 lead.

"Well, the way Wilson was throwing, you knew this was going to be a tight game," Bruce Bochy said. "Our guy was throwing well, too, and one run could be the difference. When Edgar hit the ball

Edgar Renteria was already known throughout baseball as a clutch batter, but his timely hitting in the 2010 playoffs would make him a World Series MVP and San Francisco legend.

out, you know there's a chance that that could be the game right there the way those two guys were throwing the ball. They both were on top of their game and certainly did a lot for us to get that home run because we weren't doing much off of them."

Later, when the Giants were trying to salt the game away, he hit a two-run single—mission accomplished.

"Well, Edgar has been through it," Bochy said. "Guys look up to him. He's got that leadership you like from a veteran. He's excited about playing right now. He wants to be out there, and he's really been a calming influence, I think, on everybody else in the way he plays and how he plays to win. He's really lifted this club. He's had a tough year with the injuries, but it's probably benefitted him a little bit because he's fresh. I don't know what he's going to do next year, but I will say he's playing like he wants to keep going." ■

Playing in the seventh postseason of his career, Edgar not only brought his veteran presence to the team but also the experience of what it takes to win in October and November into the club house.

Juan Uribe

Infielder's versatility, experience, and timely power prove key to Giants success

Juan Uribe knew what it felt like to play for a World Series–winning team as he played shortstop for the Chicago White Sox when they won it all in 2005.

Now he knows what it feels like to repeat the experience after being a part of the Giants group of misfits that rode team chemistry and strong pitching to a World Series championship.

Uribe began his major league career with the Colorado Rockies at the age of 21 and played three seasons for the Rockies before heading to the White Sox prior to the 2004 season. Once with the White Sox, he played second base, shortstop, third base, and center field before settling in as the starting shortstop. The following season he spent the entire season at shortstop and that's when the White Sox defeated the Houston Astros in the World Series.

Of note, Uribe made two fielding gems to end that Series. One saw him charge into the stands along the third-base line to make a catch. Then he made a snap throw on a slow roller and throw out the runner for the final out of the deciding game, thereby giving the White Sox their first title in 88 years.

Uribe signed a minor-league deal with the Giants in January of 2009 and made the team out of spring training. He has since been a pleasant surprise while playing mostly shortstop, but also some second base and third base in addition to designated hitter in American League ballparks.

While Uribe's batting average dipped in 2010 from the previous year's .289 to .248, he experienced a power surge that saw him hit 24 home runs—an increase of eight—and he went from 55 RBIs to 85. Uribe's best offensive game of the season came at a critical juncture against the Chicago Cubs on September 23 when he hit two home runs in the second inning, one of them a grand slam, giving him six RBIs in one inning.

Uribe's bat helped the Giants take two crucial games in the 2010 National League Championship Series. In Game 4, he hit a walk-off sacrifice fly and in the deciding Game 6, he hit a home run in the top of the eighth that proved to be the hit to put the Giants in the World Series.

Juan Uribe entered spring training as the team's utility infielder and ended it as a postseason hero. Playing stellar defense and having the knack for getting a hit at the right time kept Uribe in the line-up.

Cody Ross was named the NLCS MVP, but Uribe was just as deserving. Even though he had just three hits, he drove in the winning runs in two games did so while playing with a hurt left wrist, and he played stellar defense.

He continued his hot hitting in the Series by belting a three-run homer in Game 1 and driving home a run in Game 2. ■

Taking over starting duties at third base in the postseason, Uribe had some key hits that led to Giant victories—including this home run off of Darren O'Day in Game 1 of the World Series.

Giants Torture

Nothing came easy for Giants in 2010

Longtime Giants broadcaster and former second baseman Duane Kuiper came up with the descriptive phrase that would capture the Giants' most special season since moving from New York the San Francisco: "Giants torture."

On April 20, 2010, the San Diego Padres defeated the Giants 1–0 on a sacrifice fly by Scott Hairston off Jonathan Sanchez in the fourth inning. The Padres had one hit at the end of the game, yet they won their second consecutive game against the seemingly snakebitten Giants.

The following day, Kuiper, along with Mike Krukow, his partner in the booth, discussed the team's fortunes before Kuiper proclaimed, "Giants baseball." After a pause, he added: "Torture."

And the phrase caught on, particularly since it so aptly described frustrating losses as well as many of the team's wins, which always seemed to claim their pound of flesh.

Take April 28 when Tim Lincecum handcuffed the Phillies through 8-1/3 innings at AT&T Park before 32,369 Giants fans were privy to a bullpen meltdown that saw the Phillies score three in the ninth, which led to extra innings and the Phillies' eventual 7–6 win in 11 innings.

Or May 15 at AT&T Park, when Brian Wilson entered the game to try and hold a 2–1 lead over the Houston Astros. So what did the Giants closer do? He walked Pedro Feliz to start the inning before briefly recovering to strike out Humberto Quintero and retire pinch hitter Geoff Blum on a pop out. Then the inning really got interesting. Pinch hitter Cory Sullivan followed with a single and Michael Bourn walked to load the bases, bringing up Kazuo Matsui. With a crowd of 40,060 watching, Matsui fought Wilson through a 15-pitch at-bat before flying out to left, prompting Kuiper to tell his audience: "Giants beat the Astros by a final of 2–1. Giants baseball: torture."

Nothing ever comes easy for Giants fans, which seemingly made Kuiper's phrase easy to relate to.

Throughout the season, the team continued to live up to what became their motto. Each cliffhanger only added to the appropriateness of the

phrase, leading to T-shirts and signs inside the park touting the team motto.

On August 25 at AT&T Park, the Cincinnati Reds held a 10–1 lead after 4-1/2 innings, and the Giants fought back to take an 11–10 lead after eight innings only to blow the lead in the ninth to send the game into extra innings, where the Reds won 12–11 in 12 innings.

Countless examples reaffirmed the motto throughout the season. Even the players seemed to embrace "Giants Torture" in the spirit for which it was intended.

"Fans create a lot of fun things to make signs," pitcher Barry Zito said after the Giants won the National League West on the final day of the season. "However they want to play it. They were amazing the last few days. Whatever they want to focus on, we're happy, as long as they keep screaming." ■

After he and the Tampa Bay Rays parted ways early in the season, Pat Burrell joined the Giants and started producing right away. He was tied for third most homers on the team at 18, while only playing in 96 games as a Giant.

Pat Burrell

After release by Rays, outfielder solidifies Giants lineup

No player on the Giants personified the team's chemistry more than veteran Pat Burrell. Throughout the 2010 season, the Giants seemed to pick up one outcast or retread after the next only to see that player come through and become another of the seemingly endless puzzle pieces that created their championship season.

Burrell had established himself as a legitimate major league slugger during his nine seasons with the Philadelphia Phillies prior to his signing a free-agent contract with the Tampa Bay Rays after the 2008 season.

Unfortunately for Burrell and the Rays, he never seemed to adjust to his role as a designated hitter, which showed in the results accrued over parts of two seasons when he hit .218 with 16 home runs and 77 RBIs in 146 games.

"I wish I knew the answer [for what went wrong] because it probably would have worked out differently down there," Burrell said. "For me it has to have something to do with being in the flow of the game, playing in the field, being active in the game. I think that's a huge part of it for me. I'm not saying that that's right or wrong. I think just for me that was an important part of it."

On May 19, the Rays released Burrell and ten days later the Giants signed him as insurance policy, but only after he agreed to go to Triple A. The Giants were surprised he agreed to the minor-league assignment and equally surprised by what good shape he showed up in and how hard he worked. Once they finally decided to bring him to the major leagues, they initially believed he would primarily be a reserve with occasional pinch-hitting duties. But once Burrell got a chance to play, he continued to perform. He became the team's regular left fielder and came through with his bat, finishing the season with a .266 average, 18 home runs, and 56 RBIs in 96 games. In addition, he became a nice piece within the Giants' clubhouse, offering veteran leadership.

"I don't want to dwell too much on that," Burrell said when talking about his days with the Rays. "But obviously getting a chance to come out here and

Even though he struggled in the World Series, Burrell did score five runs, with four RBIs and a home run during the Giants 2010 postseason.

No player on the Giants personified the team's chemistry more than veteran Pat Burrell.

play, I think, was a big thing for me. You know, obviously starting with a different team and having it turn out the way it did is not what you hoped for. But I got a chance, the Giants gave me an opportunity to come out here and play, and I just tried to make the most of it."

Bruce Bochy allowed that Burrell had been "more than a pleasant surprise."

"Not just with his play, but also who he is, how he's helped out in that clubhouse," Bochy said. ■

Pat Burrell found redemption and a World Series ring at the end of an extraordinary 2010 season.

Brian Wilson

Bearded bullpen beast saved games, created fashion trend

Baseball fans swear they are seeing the "House of David" reincarnated every time Brian Wilson takes the mound.

Though Wilson has no ties to the barnstorming team that wore beards as they toured the country, the Giants closer fashions a heavy black beard and he is perhaps the biggest character on the team. He has also become one of the best closers in baseball.

Wilson got drafted out of LSU in the 24th round of the 2003 draft and shortly thereafter he underwent Tommy John surgery to repair his right elbow. Three years later he made his major league debut on April 23, 2006.

By 2008, Wilson had earned the role as the Giants closer and he finished that season with 41 saves. He followed the next season with 38 and he recorded 48 along with a 1.81 ERA in 2010, which went a long way toward explaining how the Giants won the National League West and stormed through the postseason to win the World Series.

Wilson uses a four-seam fastball that he can occasionally flirt with 100 mph, he also effectively employs a slider and a cut fastball, and he has great control. Perhaps most important is the fact Wilson is a competitor and has the requisite mettle to handle the ninth inning of a major league game, which brings about a situation for pitchers totally unlike anything else encountered in a nine-inning game.

Among Wilson's highlights during the Giants' championship season have been his closing out the final game of the season on October 3 against the San Diego Padres when the Giants clinched the National League West crown in addition to October 23 when he finished out Game 6 of the National League Championship Series against the Phillies, thereby sending the Giants to the World Series.

Where color is concerned, few players in baseball can compete with Wilson.

In addition to his Mohawk haircut there is the beard, which he began dying black late in the 2010 season. Wilson's beard inspired fans to begin wearing fake beards to AT&T Park and brought about the inauguration of "Fear the Beard" t-shirts.

Of note, he also chose to wear a pair of fluorescent

"Fear the Beard" and the rest of Brian Wilson too, especially if you are opposing hitters. Wilson led the major leagues in saves this year, setting a career high of 48.

orange spikes, which prompted Major League Baseball to fine him $1,000 for wearing shoes that did not conform to the dress code. His response was to use a black marker to color half of each of the orange shoes.

A little bit of crazy is always fashionable as long as the results are there, and Wilson's results are rock solid with 134 career saves along with a 3.18 ERA. Where Giants fans are concerned, watching him is one of the many reasons to go to the ballpark. ■

The Mohawk and dyed postseason beard gives Wilson an intimidating presence on the mound. His ability to paint the corners and freeze batters with his pitch repertoire makes him the dominating closer he is.

Bruce Bochy

Veteran skipper made the right calls in 2010

Bruce Bochy brought an interesting managerial style to the Giants upon joining the team as Felipe Alou's successor on October 27, 2006.

Since then, Giants fans have gotten used to seeing him shuffle the batting order, make in-game substitutions, and go against the book with pitching matchups or use of his bullpen.

Any second guessers will just have to wait to take their shots at the Giants manager after 2010 because there are no wrong calls when your club wins the World Series.

Bochy had already achieved high praise for his managerial abilities prior to taking over the Giants before the start of the 2007 season. The former major league catcher had managed the San Diego Padres for 12 seasons before signing a four-year contract with the Giants to succeed Alou.

Not only did Bochy bring a penchant for doing things his way, he also brought an interesting background.

The Giants skipper was born in Landes de Boussac, France, where his father was a U.S. Army officer. But he quickly moved stateside and grew up in Virginia before moving to Melbourne, Florida, where he attended Melbourne High School before going to Brevard Community College and Florida State University.

A strapping catcher with good size and a powerful bat, Bochy was drafted by the Houston Astros in the first round of the 1975 Major League Draft (21st overall pick). He reached the major leagues three years later, becoming one of eight major leaguers to be born in France. Unfortunately for Bochy, that would be about the only distinction he registered during his nine-year career that included stints with the Mets, Astros, and Padres. He finished with a .239 career batting average with 26 home runs in 802 career at-bats.

While the backup role may have hurt Bochy's chances to become a better player, it enhanced his knowledge of the game by watching from the bench. He became a minor league manager in the Padres organization which led to him becoming the third base coach for the major league club in 1993.

Since taking the helm in San Francisco in 2007, Bruce Bochy has helped the Giants climb from the NL West cellar to a World Series title.

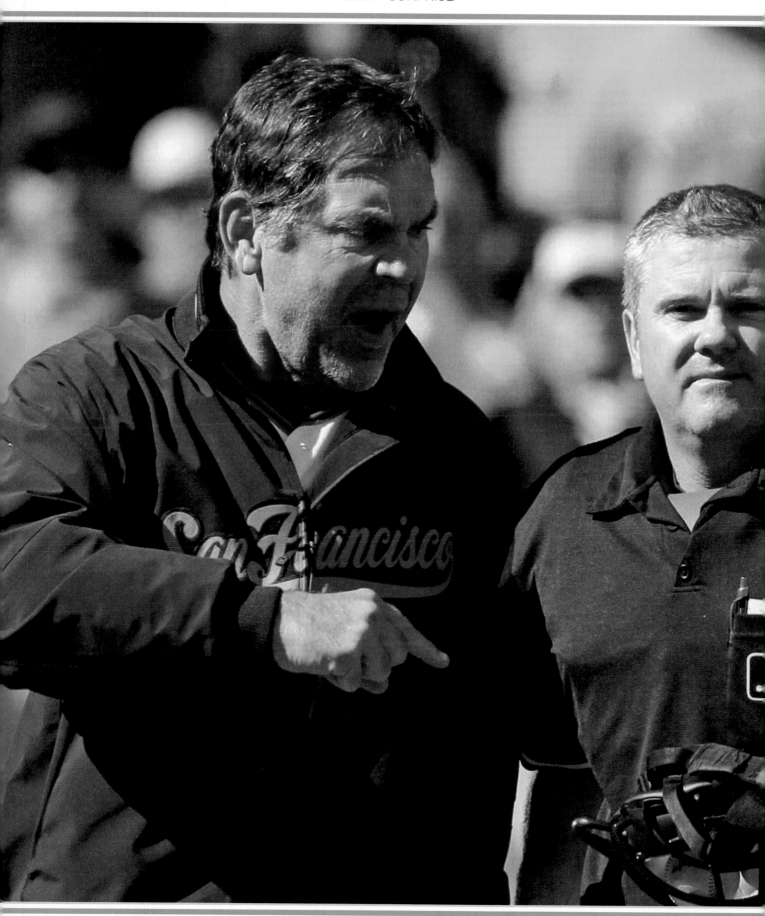

The Padres finished in last place in the National League West in 1994, which prompted the firing of manager Jim Riggleman. Bochy was promoted to take his place, making him the first former Padres player to manage the team.

In 1996, the Padres compiled the best record in the National League West and Bochy came away with National League Manager of the Year honors. Then in 1998, the Padres won 98 games en route to their second-ever appearance in the Fall Classic, where they were swept by the New York Yankees.

By the time his tenure as the Padres manager had run its course, Bochy had led the team to four postseason appearances, claiming division titles in 1996, 1998, 2005, and 2006. He won over 900 games as the Padres manager, which was quite an accomplishment based on the fact that at times the Padres fielded cost-effective teams.

Prior to the 2010 playoffs, Bochy had experienced a great deal of playoff failure as his teams lost 10 of the previous 11 postseason games he'd managed prior to 2010, when he managed a team that he has called "castoffs" and "misfits."

Bochy is known as a great communicator amongst his players, always trying to prepare them for any situation or letting them know when they might not start a game or if they are unexpectedly in the lineup.

And at the end of the 2010 season, nobody could dispute the fact that Bruce Bochy had pushed all the right buttons while guiding the Giants to their first World Series championship since 1954 and the franchise's first since moving to San Francisco in 1958. ■

Over the past two seasons, the Giants are 36 games over .500 during the regular season. Bochy's knack of filling out the lineup card has a lot to do with that mark.

Game 162

Giants 3–0 win clinches division on season's final day

A full-length major league season lasts 162 games. Rarely are all of those games needed to settle whether a team goes to the playoffs, which is what made the Giants' 162nd game of the 2010 season against the San Diego Padres so exciting: it mattered.

The Giants' last division title had come in 2003, which had also been the last season the team reached the postseason.

Three teams would be affected by the Giants' final game—the Giants, Padres, and the Atlanta Braves.

If San Diego won Game 162, the Giants, Braves, and Padres would have all finished with 91–71 records, which would have forced a tiebreaker game on the Monday following the regular season to determine the winner of the National League West. The loser would then have to play the Braves to see which team would advance to the playoffs as the NL Wild Card.

The Giants simply needed one win during their three-game series against the Padres to win the division, but that had not happened as the Padres took the first two games by scores of 6–4 and 4–2.

San Diego's pitching had been outstanding all season, so the prospect of facing rookie Mat Latos was not ideal for the Giants. The Padres right-hander brought 14 wins into the contest.

San Francisco manager Bruce Bochy sent Jonathan Sanchez to the mound to try and thrust the Giants into the playoffs with a crowd of 42,822 showing up at AT&T Park to support the home team.

Sanchez did not pick up a quality start for his work—he did not get out of the sixth inning—but the distance of the left-hander's effort did not reflect the quality of his performance as Sanchez allowed no runs on three hits while striking out five. In addition, he had effectively pitched out of trouble when he found it, retiring all five hitters he faced with runners in scoring position.

The Giants offense got going in the third when they scored two runs against Latos. Starting pitcher Sanchez helped his own cause, tripling with one out to ignite a rally that included an RBI single by Freddy Sanchez and an RBI double by Aubrey Huff.

Buster Posey padded the lead to 3–0 with a solo home run in the eighth.

After Sanchez left, the Padres continued to threaten, but five Giants relievers silenced the Padres' bats for the final four innings with closer Brian Wilson pitching an immaculate ninth to earn his 48th save of the season to nail down the 3–0 win.

Ironically, the Giants won their division on October 3, which carried historical significance for the franchise. Bobby Thomson's "Shot Heard 'Round the World" came on that date in 1951, sending the New York Giants to the World Series. Four years after moving to San Francisco, the Giants defeated the Los Angeles Dodgers in a playoff to reach the World Series on October 3, 1962.

And now, October 3, 2010, will be remembered as the date the Giants earned their place in the 2010 postseason, thereby beginning their run to their first World Championship since 1954 and their first in San Francisco. ■

The Giants avoided a one-game playoff and clinched the National League West title by beating divisional foes—and manager Bruce Bochy's former team—the San Diego Padres on the final day of the regular season.

The San Francisco Giants punched their playoff ticket by winning the National League West, defeating the San Diego Padres in the final game of the regular season. They started their postseason journey in the National League Divisional Series against the Atlanta Braves.

2010 PLAYOFFS

National League Division Series
Giants 1, Braves 0

Game 1

Lincecum strikes out 14, Ross drives in game's only run

Game 1 of the 2010 National League Division Series belonged to Tim Lincecum. After facing the Giants ace, the Atlanta Braves had to be asking themselves, "We flew across country for this?"

Lincecum got the Giants off to a 1–0 lead in the NLDS with a dominating two-hit shutout that included 14 strikeouts. However, Lincecum's start did not make anyone think of how the game would end.

Omar Infante led off the game for the Braves with 43,936 watching at AT&T Park on October 7. The Braves third baseman doubled to center field.

Lincecum had enjoyed a lot of success during his years with the Giants, but this was his first postseason start, so after Infante's hit he told himself: "Don't worry about it, make your pitches and everything will be fine. You tell yourself, you've done this a thousand times. We've been in these situations. It's another game and just treat it like that."

Lincecum then retired Jason Heyward on a fly out to left before he struck out the next two hitters to end the first inning.

In the second inning, Lincecum faced Alex Gonzales, Matt Diaz, and Brooks Conrad, overpowering the trio by striking out each. Of note, all nine of the strikes came via missed swings.

Derek Lowe started for the Braves and looked to be up to the task as the game moved into the bottom of the fourth in the midst of a scoreless tie. Buster Posey singled to lead off the bottom of the fourth. When Pat Burrell struck out swinging, Posey took off for second and successfully collected the first stolen base of his major league career. Replays made umpire Paul Emmel's call look questionable, to which Posey quipped after the game: "I guess it's a good thing we don't have instant replay."

The Giants weren't about to look a gift horse in the mouth.

After Juan Uribe struck out for the second out and Pablo Sandoval was intentionally walked, Cody Ross singled to left field to score Posey for the only

Tim Lincecum set the tone for the rest of the Giants pitching staff by hurling a complete game shutout in Game 1 of the NLDS.

"Don't worry about it, make your pitches and everything will be fine."

—Tim Lincecum to himself before taking the mound for his first-ever postseason start against the Braves.

run of the game. Lincecum issued an intentional walk to Jason Heyward in the fourth then he proceeded to retire the next 10 hitters and he retired 18 of the final 19 batters he faced.

Lincecum's performance set the franchise postseason strikeout record. The previous record stood at 10 and was shared by Jesse Barnes, Carl Hubbell, Hal Schumacher, and Jack Sanford.

The final pitch of Lincecum's 119-pitch outing registered at 92 miles per hour. Derek Lee took the pitch for strike three and AT&T Park went berserk as the Giants had their first win of the postseason under their belts.

"He was lights out," Braves manager Bobby Cox said. "We had two runners at second base the whole night, and that was it. I don't know how many he struck out, but it was more than fingers on my hand."

Lincecum did not have as good a season in 2010 as his previous two Cy Young years, but Giants manager Bruce Bochy kept the faith in his right-hander.

"I could see Timmy having a night like this," Bochy said. "We never lost confidence in this kid, and I've said this many times, we all have our ups and downs, and he was searching there for a little while, but he found it. And he's been on a nice roll here. And he said some—he's had some rest, and it showed tonight. And he went out there and pitched as fine of a ballgame as you can pitch." ■

The Freak definitely did not let the Atlanta Braves hitters feel at home in Game 1. Lincecum allowed only two hits while striking out 14 batters in the series opener.

National League Division Series
Giants 4, Braves 5

Game 2

Ankiel's 11th inning homer evens series as teams head to Atlanta

Everything appeared to be going the Giants' way in Game 2 of the National League Championship Series.

AT&T Park felt vibrant as the 44,046 fans watching cheered the home team as they carried a 4–0 lead into the sixth inning with Matt Cain on the mound and pitching well. Added all up, the Giants appeared well on their way to a commanding 2–0 lead in the best-of-five series.

Though the Giants didn't need to be reminded of the fact that all 27 outs need to be accounted for before a game is complete, before the 27th out was made, the Braves reminded the Giants of that fact.

Six outs from the finish line, the Giants began to come undone.

Sergio Romo started the eighth for the Giants and allowed two singles, prompting manager Bruce Bochy to bring in closer Brian Wilson. Wilson had not converted a two-inning save all season, but Bochy thought the time was right.

"Game was on the line there," Bochy said. "You know, they had some good pinch hitters up there, and once you got a couple of guys on, we got a day off tomorrow, Wilson hasn't pitched in a while, and we've got five outs from them, but at that point we want to stop them."

Unfortunately for the Giants, Wilson performed his job against the first batter he faced, Melky Cabrera, who hit a weak grounder to third. Pablo Sandoval fielded the ball, but he threw wild to Aubrey Huff at first. The error allowed a run to score and by the time the eighth had run its course, the Braves had scored three runs to tie the game at four.

The game went to extra innings and the Giants seemed to have matters under control when they loaded the bases with one out in the 10th. That's when Buster Posey grounded into a double play to set up a dramatic ending for the Braves.

With one out in the 11th inning and Ramon Ramirez on the mound for the Giants, Rick Ankiel

Courtesy of an early Pat Burrell home run, the Giants jumped out to an early lead in Game 2 of the NLDS. Unfortunately for the Giants, the lead didn't hold.

"Wilson hasn't pitched in a while, and we've got five outs...but at that point we want to stop them."

—Manager Bruce Bochy on his ill-fated decision to bring Brian Wilson in for a two-inning save for the first time all season.

homered on a 2–2 pitch to right field to give the Braves a 5–4 lead.

Ramirez is "tough," Ankiel said. "I feel like he likes to use the split along with his fastball. So I tried to get a good pitch to swing at, and I got a good fastball. I put good wood on it and a good thing happened."

Kyle Farnesworth shut down the Giants in the bottom of the 11th and just like that, the Giants had squandered a big lead and a 1–0 lead in the series to face a road trip to Atlanta. The odds had suddenly shifted in the Braves' favor.

Since the beginning of Division Series play in 1995, teams from both leagues had gained a split on the road in the first two games 11 times and in eight of those series those teams had won.

Given the baggage the Giants faced from past playoff failures, the team had their work cut out for them as the series headed east. ■

The San Francisco faithful had to endure the "torture" when the Giants ended up dropping Game 2 of the NLDS in extra innings to the Atlanta Braves.

National League Division Series
Giants 3, Braves 2

Game 3

Giants overcome late homer, Braves ninth-inning error allows go-ahead run to score

After losing Game 2 of the 2010 National League Division Series late in the game, there were questions about how the Giants would react if a similar situation developed during the playoffs.

That answer would come in October 10 when the Division Series moved east to Atlanta, where 53,284 watched at Turner Field.

Jonathan Sanchez started for the Giants and brought to mind memories of Tim Lincecum and Matt Cain while he carved up the Braves' lineup. The Giants left-hander had allowed no runs and just one hit, striking out 11 Braves hitters as the game headed into the eighth inning.

But when Alex Gonzalez led off the eighth with a single on Sanchez's 105th pitch of the game, Giants manager Bruce Bochy had a decision to make: Leave Sanchez in or go with Sergio Romo, who had allowed back-to-back singles upon entering Game 2.

While making his decision, Bochy could see right-handed hitting Troy Glaus in the on-deck circle. Thus, Bochy signaled for Romo.

Retiring Braves skipper Bobby Cox countered the move by replacing Glaus with left-handed hitting Eric Hinske, who hit a 2–2 slider from Romo into the right-field stands to give the Braves a 2–1 lead.

"We thought, or I did, that Sanchez was at that point," Bochy said, explaining his move. "I mean, what a job he did. It didn't work out. That's not a good feeling when you make a change and they hit a two-run homer. But the pen's done a great job all year. We have a lot of confidence in them. Serge just made a mistake there, got the ball up, and they took advantage of it.

"But I just felt that Sanchy had done his job, he was at that point, and we had a fresh pen down there and give them credit."

Suddenly the Giants were facing the prospect of finding themselves down 2–1 in the Division Series,

In Game 3, Freddy Sanchez scored the winning run in the top of the ninth on a ball put into play by Aubrey Huff. The 3–2 win over Atlanta gave the Giants a 2–1 lead in the series.

"They hit the home run they needed, but...what was important is how we handled it. We came right back and found a way to get a couple of runs."
—Manager Bruce Bochy

one game away from elimination.

Romo did not cave after surrendering the home run and allowed no further damage in the eighth. The Giants offense then got busy in the ninth.

Right-hander Craig Kimbrel started the ninth for the Braves and the rookie retired Cody Ross on a pop out to second base. Travis Ishikawa then drew a walk on a 3–2 pitch. Kimbrel then struck out Andres Torres for the second out before getting ahead of Freddy Sanchez 0–2, leaving the Braves one strike away from a win.

Sanchez worked the count to 1–2 before he singled to center, bringing Aubrey Huff to the plate, which prompted Cox to bring in left-hander Mike Dunn.

Huff had recorded only two hits in his first 11 at-bats of the NLDS, but he had been one of the Giants' better clutch hitters during the regular season, and he hit left-handers almost as well as he hit right-handers.

Huff watched a 95 mph fastball for strike one before dropping in a single to right field. Ishikawa scored on the hit to tie the game at two.

"[Dunn is] one of the toughest lefties in the league, if you ask me, out of the pen," Huff said. "I faced Dunn at our place, and he threw me five straight sliders. First pitch I was looking slider, put it right down the middle at 95. Kind of kicking myself a little bit. But stayed with it, saw it, and was able to reach out there and get it. It was a pretty good pitch.

"Just kind of hit it off the end a tad enough to where it could get down. When I hit it, it was the longest fly ball, medium fly ball I've ever hit. I didn't think it was ever going to get down. But they were probably playing no doubles, or they might catch it."

Braves second baseman Brooks Conrad, who had already made two errors in the game, allowed a shot by Buster Posey to go through his legs for his third error of the game. Sanchez scored on the play to give the Giants a 3–2 lead.

Brian Wilson came in to pitch the ninth and recorded the final three outs of the game to preserve the 3–2 win.

"They hit the home run they needed, but, again, what was important is how we handled it," Bochy said. "We came right back and found a way to get a couple of runs." ■

It was Jonathan Sanchez's gem of a start that put the Giants offense in position to win Game 3. Over 7-1/3 innings pitched, he gave up only two hits and one earned run while striking out 11 batters.

National League Division Series
Giants 3, Braves 2

Game 4

Ross leads the way as Giants overcome Lowe, Braves to move on to NLCS

Chalk this one up to Cody Ross. Game 4 of the 2010 National League Division Series was decided by Ross' bat as he led the Giants to a 3–2 win over the Atlanta Braves with 44,532 watching at Turner Field.

Ross had a home run and an RBI single to help the Giants advance to the National League Championship Series.

The baseball played during the NLDS wasn't cut from the Spalding Guide as it got sloppy at times—both teams combined for 10 errors, and the hitting wasn't the kind that would have prompted Ted Williams to spew superlatives. The Giants hit .212 and the Braves hit .175. But the games were exciting and closely played as all of the four games were decided by one run.

And Ross—a role player throughout his career—made the difference in the clinching game.

Derek Lowe started for the Braves and he brought along some quality stuff even though he was pitching on three days' rest. The Braves right-hander took a no-hitter into the sixth inning when he faced Ross with one out and the Braves leading 1–0.

"Derek was outstanding tonight," Ross said. "He wasn't making any mistakes. Our game plan going in was to try to get his pitch count up and try to work him and try to get him out of the game early. He wasn't having it. He was going in, pounding the zone and pitched an outstanding game.

"So after my first at-bat, he made me look pretty bad. I just went up there and said I'm going to try to be aggressive and look for something to hit early. And right before that, actually, Edgar Renteria told me: 'Cody, get your foot down. You're not getting your foot down.' And I went and watched my video after my bat. And he was right, I wasn't. So I tried to get it down early, got a pitch I could handle and luckily got some good wood on it."

Ross sent a line drive to left field that just did

Brian Wilson picked up his second postseason save to end Game 4, securing the Giants their spot in the National League Championship Series.

"We were fortunate to have come out on top. We know it. We knew we had our hands full."

—Manager Bruce Bochy on the series win over the Braves.

clear the wall to break up the no-hit bid and tie the game at 1.

Madison Bumgarner started for the Giants and got victimized twice by Brian McCann, who had a sacrifice fly in the third to give Atlanta a 1–0 lead then he homered off Bumgarner in the sixth to put the Braves up 2–1.

Ross then answered in the top of the seventh when he stepped to the plate with the bases loaded and the score tied at 2. This time Ross faced reliever Jonny Venters, and he delivered a single to left to score the go-ahead run and give the Giants a 3–2 lead.

Santiago Casilla and Javier Lopez held the Braves scoreless in the seventh and eighth innings before Brian Wilson came in to pitch the ninth. However, the final out did not come without some final dramatics.

Wilson walked two to put runners at first and second with one out, giving the Braves two chances to drive home the tying run. But Wilson recovered to strike out Omar Infante before he retired Melky Cabrera on a ground out to end the game.

Bumgarner picked up the win, making him the youngest pitcher in Giants history to win a postseason game at age 21.

While the Giants celebrated on the field, they suddenly stopped their celebration to make one of the more classy gestures seen in sports when they stopped what they were doing to salute Cox by applauding the retiring Braves manager.

Shortly thereafter, the Giants were back in the clubhouse drinking champagne for the second time in nine days after earning a spot in the National League Championship Series.

"This series had everything," Bruce Bochy said. "You know, the errors, we hit one today. That's going to happen. But just the intensity and excitement of the series, it had to be thrilling for the fans. There was never an easy moment for Bobby or myself, because these games could have gone either way.

"We were fortunate to have come out on top. We know it. We knew we had our hands full with the pitching. We're fortunate to have outstanding pitching, too, and what a job they did. That young kid, Bumgarner, I mean, his first postseason game, and you wouldn't know it the way he handled himself, and that's why I let him hit after we tied the game. He gave up the home run, settled down, and pitched great. It was just a great series, I think. If you're a baseball fan, you had to love this series." ∎

In one of the classiest moves ever seen on a baseball field, the Giants paused mid-celebration to congratulate Braves manager Bobby Cox on a terrific career. Cox retired from baseball after the NLDS loss with a .556 winning percentage at the helm of the Braves.

National League Championship Series
Giants 4, Phillies 3

Game 1

Lincecum, Ross too much for Phillies as Giants take opener

The Phillies were looking to return to the World Series for a third consecutive season—and Philadelphia appeared to have a stronger team than in their previous two trips to the Fall Classic. So the Giants were clearly underdogs entering this one.

Particularly when the Phillies had a trio of starting pitchers that included Roy Halladay, Cole Hamels, and Roy Oswalt.

But as the old saying goes, that's why they play the games.

In Game 1 of the National League Championship Series, the Phillies sent ace Roy Halladay to the mound and the Giants countered with their own ace, Tim Lincecum. A crowd of 45,929 at Philly's Citizens Bank Park watched what most figured would be a classic pitching duel.

As he had during the Giants' win over the Atlanta Braves in the National League Division Series, Cody Ross once again stole the show, stating his case to be recognized as the best late-season pickup in Giants history. Most players are lucky to get a hit against Halladay and some of the more blessed manage to hit a home run against the veteran right-hander. Ross hit two home runs against Halladay, the pitcher many believe to be the best in the major leagues.

Ross' first came in the top of the third inning with one out to stake the Giants to a 1–0 lead. In the top of the fifth, he again homered to again establish a Giants' lead at 2–1.

"In the past I've tried everything against them, trying to wait them out and be aggressive, and I guess in between there and just trying to look for a pitch to drive, luckily I got it," said Ross, who was in the lineup for the Florida Marlins the night Halladay twirled a perfect game against them. "I'm just trying to hit something in the hole, trying to find a hole and luckily got some good wood on it and got it up in the air."

Cody Ross put San Francisco's offense on his back in Game 1 of the NLCS, taking Phillies ace Roy Halladay deep twice on the way to a Giants 4-3 victory.

Halladay allowed four earned runs on eight hits in seven innings while striking out seven and walking one.

"The first pitch to Ross I didn't think was that bad; the second one, I left the ball over the plate," Halladay said. "In the sixth, a couple pitches cost me. At this point, if you make a couple mistakes, they end up costing you."

While Ross' home runs were big, veteran Pat Burrell's RBI double and Juan Uribe's RBI single in the sixth pushed the Giants' lead to 4–1.

"When he started me off with a fastball I believe and I got behind 0–2 again and just really trying to get something to put a good swing on, keep the inning going, that was kind of our plan against him today, was to keep the line moving," Burrell said. "We got a lot of guys that are capable of doing damage; they're power threats. But off a guy like this, we have to make a conscious effort to tone it down and get good pitches to hit, which still isn't easy."

The runs in the sixth could not have come at a better time since Jayson Werth hit a two-run homer off Lincecum in the bottom half of the inning to cut the Giants' lead to 4–3 with three innings remaining.

Lincecum gutted out one more inning before handing off the baseball to Javier Lopez to start the eighth. Lopez retired Chase Utley on a groundout and struck out Ryan Howard, prompting Bruce Bochy to bring in closer Brian Wilson to try and get the final three outs.

"Willie has shown the ability to get four or five outs," Bochy said. "He's had a lot of rest. We're in a one-run ballgame, so I brought my best, my closer in there. That's what I will do."

After giving up a single to Werth, Wilson struck out Jimmy Rollins to end the eighth. Wilson then got the final three outs in the ninth, hitting one batter and striking out the other three to end the game and preserve the Giants' 4–3 win to give them a 2–1 lead in the series. ∎

Right fielder Nate Schierholtz, who entered the game for Pat Burrell as a pinch runner, congratulates Cody Ross on his big night during the Giants celebration after Game 1 in Philadelphia.

107

National League Championship Series
Giants 1, Phillies 6

Game 2

Oswalt continues postseason dominance as Phillies even series

Jimmy Rollins experienced a tough season for the Phillies in 2010, playing in just 88 games due to hamstring and calf problems.

After what amounted to a less than desirable regular season for the former National League Most Valuable Player, Rollins got off to a bad start in the playoffs—collecting just one hit in 15 trips to the plate.

But that didn't stop Rollins from taking care of business in the Phillies' 6–1 win over the Giants in Game 2 of the National League Championship Series.

In the bottom of the first inning, Giants starter Jonathan Sanchez helped out the Phillies by experiencing control problems. He walked three batters, including Rollins, who drove home the game's first run with his free pass to give the Phillies a 1–0 lead. Sanchez threw 35 pitches that inning but managed to keep his cool and he escaped the first by allowing just one run and another in the fifth, leaving the Giants trailing 2–1 after six innings.

Unfortunately for the Giants, Rollins had not sufficiently whetted his appetite.

Facing Santiago Casilla in the bottom of the seventh with the bases loaded, Rollins unloaded on a fastball and drove ball to the top of the wall in right-center field for a double that emptied the bases while blowing open the game en route to a 6–1 Phillies win.

"It was something that was needed at the time," said Rollins of his double. "I was glad I was the person up there at the moment and able to come through. But you don't celebrate until you win four games. And once we get to that point, then you can look back and say that was a big hit, but for now, just gave us a little breathing room, a chance to go into San Francisco 1–1 and get the win."

Cody Ross again did his part with a solo home run off Phillies starter Roy Oswalt with one out in the fifth, but that would prove to be the Giants' only run on the night.

Oswalt allowed one run on three hits in eight

Jonathan Sanchez took the mound for the start of Game two in Philadelphia. He allowed two earned runs over six innings pitched while striking out seven Phillies, but it wasn't good enough to secure a win.

"He threw really great.... He's a really good pitcher. He was on tonight."

—Manager Bruce Bochy on Phillies starting pitcher Roy Oswalt

innings of work before handing the ball over to Ryan Madson, who safely navigated the ninth to preserve the win.

"I had a real good run on the ball tonight," Oswalt said. "Seemed like I could throw through the outside part of the plate real well to lefties and keep it away from them and kind of run it across the plate.

"I tried to stay mainly fastball most of the game, tried to make some changeups here, and toward the end of the game started to get the curveball back, and threw few of those pretty well in the last part of the game."

Giants manager Bruce Bochy felt like he had seen a masterpiece by Oswalt.

"He threw really great," Bochy said. "He's a really good pitcher. He was on tonight. He had his stuff and we had our work cut out. And Sanchez I thought he threw well. He struggled early in the first inning with his command, but he gave us a chance. But their guy was on and pitched very well tonight."

While the Giants would have liked to have swept the two games in Philadelphia, splitting was the next best thing and fueled the club with optimism as they headed to San Francisco to play the middle three games of the NLCS. ■

The red hot Cody Ross is congratulated as he enters the dugout after his fifth-inning home run off of Roy Oswalt. His solo shot accounted for the only run the Giants scored in Game 2.

National League Championship Series
Giants 3, Phillies 0

Game 3

Cain, Giants hand Hamels first career NLCS loss

Facing their third ace in three games against the Phillies in Game 3 of the 2010 National League Championship Series, the Giants took a 3–0 win over the Phillies as the Series shifted to San Francisco, where an AT&T Park crowd of 43,320 watched.

After facing the likes of Roy Halladay and Roy Oswalt in Games 1 and 2, the Giants faced tough left-hander Cole Hamels, who appeared to be up to the task right out of the chute when he went through the Giants' lineup without an interruption and appeared headed for a special day.

Edgar Renteria finally broke the silence in the fourth with a single to right. Two outs later, Pat Burrell drew a walk. Cody Ross then came through with a single to left to score Renteria.

"Renteria did a great job by starting us off," Ross said. "And Burrell came up and had a big at-bat and drew a walk. And I was just trying to stay calm and got a pitch that probably wasn't very good

pitch to hit but ended up getting some good wood on it, and luckily it got enough and it went out in the outfield, and we pushed one across."

Aubrey Huff drove home Burrell with a single to put the Giants up 2–0.

In the fifth, Aaron Rowand got things started for the Giants with a leadoff double and he scored on Freddy Sanchez's single to push the lead to 3–0.

All told, Hamels was charged with three earned runs on five Giants hits—of which four were singles—while he struck out eight and walked one to take his first take his first-ever loss in the NLCS, moving to a record of 3–1.

Meanwhile, Matt Cain started for the Giants and had everything going for him, including good stuff.

Through 7-2/3 innings, Cain had shut out the Phillies when he walked pinch-hitter Ross Gload with his 110th pitch of the game. Shane Victorino was the next Phillies hitter, prompting a mound visit from Giants manager Bruce Bochy.

With the series moving to San Francisco in Game 3, starter Matt Cain didn't disappoint the hometown crowd. He threw seven innings of shutout baseball while allowing only two hits.

"To be able to pitch in the postseason is great, and to be able to throw the ball well and help your team win is a great feeling."
—Starting pitcher Matt Cain

"Really, more than anything I just wanted to check on him, to see where he was at," Bochy said. "He worked pretty hard. The pitch count was up there. That was his last hitter, and somehow he found a way to get a big out for us."

Cain said his manager, "Just asked me how I was feeling."

"Just kind of instilling some confidence in me," Cain said. "It didn't sound like he wanted to take me out of the game. He wanted me to make my pitches and get that guy out."

Victorino grounded out to second base on Cain's 119th pitch of the game to end the threat and basically wrap up Game 3.

"When [Cain] was in trouble he got even better, it seemed like," Phillies manager Charlie Manuel said. "I thought Cain was too good. He didn't give us any runs."

By winning, the Giants took a 2–1 advantage in the NLCS, which moved the odds into their favor. In the 19 previous times that the NLCS had stood at 2–1 after three games, the team holding the 2–1 advantage had won 15 times.

"This guy, he's incredible to do what he did today against their lineup going eight shutout. He got himself in a couple of jams and worked his way out of it and that's what you want when you're coming back home off a split, you want a guy like Cain who has no fear and go out there and do what he did," Ross said of Cain's performance. "Don't take anything away from Cole. He threw amazing as well. He was hitting his spots and throwing well, and we just—we got lucky and scored a couple of runs early. And Matt held them for the remainder. And our bullpen came in, did an outstanding job."

Cain ranked his performance at the top for his career.

"To be able to pitch in the postseason is great, and to be able to throw the ball well and help your team win is a great feeling," Cain said. ■

Aaron Rowand received his first start of the postseason against lefty Cole Hamels in Game 3 of the NLCS. He finished the day 1-3 with a run scored in the Giants 3-0 victory.

National League Championship Series
Giants 6, Phillies 5

Game 4

Uribe's late-inning magic puts Giants on the brink

A new hero seems to step forward every game when all is well. Game 4 just happened to be Juan Uribe's turn for the Giants when they took a commanding 3–1 series lead in the 2010 National League Championship Series.

Uribe did not start due to a bruised left wrist, but that injured wrist did not stop him from becoming the hero of the game when he got the chance.

With the score tied at five entering the ninth inning, Uribe was inserted into the game as a defensive replacement as part of a double-switch with Giants closer Brian Wilson. Despite barely having the chance to warm up, Uribe made an immediate impact while making manager Bruce Bochy look like a genius.

Ross Gload unleashed a hard grounder leading off the ninth that put Uribe in the awkward position of having to backpedal to field it. Once the Giants shortstop had the ball, he somehow managed to snap off a throw while falling away that reached first baseman Aubrey Huff's glove in time to nip Gload for the first out.

In the bottom half of the inning, Huff and Buster Posey cobbled together back-to-back singles putting runners at the corners with one out and Uribe stepping to the plate.

Uribe's sore wrist brought more concerns when he hit than when he played in the field, but Bochy had gotten a good report from Uribe prior to the game.

"He took BP, said it felt a lot better," Bochy said. "He said he was available and we checked on him again late in the ballgame. If [Brian Wilson] had a fairly easy inning, he was going back out there for two innings, we made a double-switch. I felt comfortable putting Juan out there."

The count moved to 1–1 when a fastball by Roy Oswalt rode in on Uribe, who maintained the pitch had hit him. Wally Bell did not share Uribe's view, and the home-plate umpire called the pitch strike two. Bochy briefly argued the call before returning

Freddy Sanchez got the scoring started in the bottom of the first inning on a Buster Posey double. This would just be the first of 11 combined runs scored in this very exciting back-and-forth game.

to the dugout, leaving Uribe to face the music against one of the Phillies' three aces, who could particularly toy with a hitter when ahead in the count. Uribe fouled off two pitches before getting just enough of a 1–2 changeup to send the ball far enough into left field to score Huff with the winning run.

"We had the right guy at the plate there, and he's come through so many times for us and got a ball he could handle to get deep enough in the outfield," Bochy said.

While Uribe's hit proved to be the winner, Posey had a memorable night with four hits in five trips to the plate, which included two doubles and two RBIs.

"What a great night he had," Bochy said. "He did all the damage for us, really. I mean, to get that big hit, it's quite a night, every at-bat he delivered for us and he's a talent. We know it. We've seen it for a while and he certainly came through tonight for us, two-out hits. Big hit there in the last inning.

"Nothing he does surprises me. Since we brought him up he played great baseball, both sides of the ball receiving, swinging the bat. He's a guy that we, it's obvious we think a lot of. He's our No. 1 pick and brought him up here. We turned it over to him, and he's done a great job. But it's fun to watch this kid play. It really is. The month he had in July, he carried us, and he's a guy you want up there and he finds a way to get it done." ∎

After making a dazzling play in the top of the ninth, Juan Uribe played hero with the bat in the bottom of the frame. On a 1-2 pitch from Roy Oswalt, Uribe sent a sacrifice fly into left field that scored Aubrey Huff from third for the winning run.

National League Championship Series
Giants 2, Phillies 4

Game 5

Halladay too much for Giants as Phillies avoid elimination

Closing out a team is one of the hardest maneuvers to execute in the postseason. Blocking the Giants' road to the World Series in Game 5 of the National League Championship Series was a major obstacle in Roy Halladay.

Despite Halladay pitching through a pulled groin, the Phillies ace managed to give his team enough to get through six innings and lead to a 4–2 win over the Giants with 43,713 watching at AT&T Park.

In the second inning, Halladay experienced pain in his right leg while delivering a pitch to Cody Ross. Despite the injury, diagnosed as a groin pull, Halladay did not leave the game. Instead he did everything he could do to stay on the mound.

Hoping to prevent having his leg tighten up, he rode a stationary bike in between innings and shortened his stride on the mound, which relieved some of the stress on the injured groin.

"I felt like it was something I could get by with," Halladay said.

Somehow Halladay made it work.

Tim Lincecum started for the Giants and his teammates staked him to a 1–0 lead after Phillies second baseman Chase Utley failed to complete an inning-ending double play. Add Halladay's wounded status to that beginning and Giants fans began to anticipate a big celebration at AT&T Park.

But the longer the game continued and the Giants let Halladay grow accustomed to his new constraints, the Phillies seemed to gather strength. The defending National League champions would not go gently into that good night.

Raul Ibanez singled to lead off the Phillies' half of the third inning before Lincecum hit Ruiz with a pitch. Halladay then bunted, producing a dud that rolled just past home plate. Buster Posey pounced on the ball and threw quickly to third, but Pablo Sandoval missed the base with his leg. Since Halladay did not even attempt to run on the play, Sandoval threw to first to get Halladay. Nevertheless, Halladay

In a rematch of Game 1 aces, Tim Lincecum's solid start of three runs allowed, two earned, over seven innings with seven strikeouts was not enough for a Giants win.

"When you're going against a good team like this, you have to play your best ball."
—Manager Bruce Bochy on playing the Phillies

had achieved his mission by getting the runners into scoring position with one out.

"Actually, it [was] a bad bunt," Bruce Bochy said. "And they got a break there. Buster did a great job giving it to Pablo. He just couldn't find the bag and fell down there.

But we're inches away from getting a double play and the bunt was right in front of home plate. At that point the third baseman goes back to the bag and we had a force there, and he wasn't running. So that's a missed opportunity for us not getting the double play, and it came back to haunt us."

More times than not, a botched play will lead to bigger things and that's exactly what happened to the Giants. Shane Victorino followed with a wicked grounder to the right side of the infield that Aubrey Huff could not come up with at first base. The ball ricocheted into center field, allowing Ibanez and Ruiz to score. Placido Polanco then laced a single to center to score Victorino to give the Phillies a 3–1 lead.

Mistakes are, "Going to happen," Bochy said. "These guys have been doing a great job on defense. And we're playing a really good club that you can't give extra outs to. And the other game we lost, we played a little sloppy there, too. And when you're going against a good team like this, you have to play your best ball. We had a hiccup in that inning and gave them some extra outs and it came back to get us."

The Giants got one back in the fourth to cut the lead to 3–2, but that would be it against Halladay.

Jose Contreras and J.C. Romero combined to pitch a scoreless seventh, Ryan Madson struck out the side in the eighth, and Brad Lidge finished off the Giants with an immaculate effort in the ninth.

Obviously, the outcome of the game disappointed the San Francisco faithful as they wanted to celebrate a National League pennant on their own turf; Bochy remained the calm voice of reason.

"With this club, as you know, we don't do anything easy," Bochy said. "And what they've been through, they'll put this behind us. And, believe me, under no illusion did we think this was going to be easy playing a great club. So we took the series here and got close to getting it tonight. Just made a couple mistakes. But we'll put this behind us and fly out tomorrow and get ready for the next game." ■

Chase Utley, chasing down the Giants' Freddy Sanchez here, diffused a potential Giants rally in the seventh inning when he made a great defensive play at second base on an Aubrey Huff line drive to end the inning.

National League Championship Series
Giants 3, Phillies 2

Game 6

Uribe's home run launches Giants into World Series

From the manner in which Game 6 of the National League Championship Series began, the Giants appeared to be suffering from a hangover from Game 5 when they could not close out the Phillies.

Jonathan Sanchez started Game 6 for the Giants and could not get the job done, allowing two runs through two innings before walking Placido Polanco to start the third, then hitting Chase Utley in the back. A tense moment followed when Utley flipped the ball back at Sanchez. Words were exchanged between the two, but no punches were thrown and order was quickly restored.

"I call it two teams who really want it bad," Giants reliever Javier Lopez said. "Utley's one of the best players in the game. He wants it as bad as anybody else and he showed it there."

Despite the fact the Giants still led the series 3–2, many figured that the Giants' Cinderella story would end once the NLCS moved back to Philadelphia where the Giants would have to face Roy Oswalt and Cole Hamels. What most did not know was the urgency in which Bochy had decided he would play the game.

After yanking Sanchez, Bochy called on a succession of three straight lefties to enter the game in the form of Jeremy Affeldt, Madison Bumgarner, and Lopez. The lefty troika held the Phillies scoreless for five innings to take the Giants through seven innings.

In the top of the third, Aubrey Huff singled home one run and scored on an error to tie the score at two and that's where the game stood when the Giants took their turn to bat in the eighth.

Pat Burrell grounded out against Ryan Madson to start the inning and Cody Ross followed with a fly out to left to bring up Juan Uribe. Madson had not been scored against during the NLCS and appeared to be continuing that trend in Game 6 until he opted to throw a cutter to Uribe on the first pitch. Uribe

Juan Uribe was the hero at the plate again, while the bullpen did its job in Game 6, to give the San Francisco Giants their first trip to the World Series since 2002.

"I've never squeezed the ball harder and never lobbed the ball softer to second base."

—Aubrey Huff on completing a key play to help the Giants clinch the 2010 National League pennant.

swung at the pitch and planted the ball into the front row in right field for a home run and a 3–2 lead.

Bochy wasn't about to get conservative at this point, so he called for The Freak to start the bottom of the eighth.

Tim Lincecum entered the game and got the first out of the inning when Jayson Werth struck out swinging. Shane Victorino and Raul Ibanez followed with singles, putting the tying run at second base. Bochy had seen enough and decided the time was right to go to closer Brian Wilson.

Carlos Ruiz stepped to the plate and the count went to 1–1 when Ruiz hit a line drive that found Huff and he threw to second base to double off Victorino to end the threat.

"I've never squeezed the ball harder and never lobbed the ball softer to second base," Huff said.

The Giants loaded the bases with two out in the ninth, but Brad Lidge retired Wilson on a groundout to end the threat.

Wilson returned to the mound in the bottom of the ninth and issued a one-out walk to Jimmy Rollins. Polanco then hit into a force out before Utley walked to put runners at first and second.

Ryan Howard stepped to the plate and the crowd of 46,062 at Citizens Bank Park howled for the slugger to come through. But Wilson was just a little better on this night. Howard took a 3–2 cut fastball at the knees for strike three and home-plate umpire Tom Hallion rang him up for the final out of the game.

Suddenly the Giants were National League champions.

"The Giants have a good team," Utley said. "They played well, and I think they're going to represent the National League very well."

Phillies manager Charlie Manuel said his team had chances but they could not "cash in on them."

"We couldn't get the big hit," Manuel said. "I talk about it every night during the season. Every night I say basically the same thing about like the team gets the big hit or makes a pitch or actually makes a play, especially late in the game where the games are tied or one-run game or things like that, those are usually the teams that win. Tonight the game was traveling there. And what's his name, the shortstop, he hit a home run there on a fastball out away from him, looked like a fastball and that was a big blow there late in the game. And that stood up."

"We had a chance, felt like Ruiz made the line drive and turned into a double play, but that's something—that's baseball and that's the way it goes and it's hard to explain sometimes. Yeah, it was a good game, but at the same time we come out on the short end of the stick, and they deserved to win."

After a celebration on the field that lasted just over five minutes, the Giants carried over their celebration into the visiting clubhouse where beer and champagne flowed.

"Any time you take down the champs, it's a good feeling," Affeldt said. "They say to be the best you have to beat the best. And we did in this series."

Cody Ross was voted the Most Valuable Player of the NLCS after hitting .350 with three home runs, five RBIs, and a .950 slugging percentage.

"We get a lot of family and friends telling us we give them heart attacks with these games," Giants second baseman Freddy Sanchez said. "But I think we've been prepared for these games, we had them all year. We have a lot of heroes, a lot of guys that just want to win and everyone steps up." ■

Brian Wilson celebrates his five-out save to win Game 6 with his signature salute after striking out Ryan Howard looking to end the game and send the Giants to the World Series.

Edgar Renteria hoists the trophy awarded to the World Series MVP after the Giants victory in Game 5.